Today I Will Do One Thing

Today I Will Do One Thing

*Daily Readings for Recovery
from Addiction and
Mental Health Disorders*

TIM Mᶜ

Hazelden
Publishing

Hazelden Publishing
Center City, Minnesota 55012
hazelden.org/bookstore

Library of Congress Cataloging-in-Publication Data

Mᶜ, Tim.
    Today i will do one thing / Tim Mᶜ
        p. cm.
    Includes index.
    ISBN 978-1-56838-083-4
    1. Dual diagnosis—Meditations. 2. Twelve Step programs.
    3. Self-help techniques. 4. Affirmations. I. Title.

    RC564.68.M3 1995
    616.86′0651—dc20
                                                    95-1887
CIP

Editor's note

Hazelden Betty Ford Foundation offers a variety of information on addiction and
related areas. Our publications do not necessarily represent Hazelden Betty Ford's
programs, nor do they officially speak for any Twelve Step organization.

In the process of being reissued in 2021, *Today I Will Do One Thing* has under-
gone minor editing updates and been retypeset in the Whitman font family.

To the greatest degree possible, the accuracy of quotations and sources has
been verified.

25 24 23 22   2 3 4 5 6

TYPESETTING: PERCOLATOR GRAPHIC DESIGN
DEVELOPMENTAL EDITOR: CATHY BROBERG
EDITORIAL PRODUCTION MANAGER: BETTY CHRISTIANSEN

To my family of origin with love:

Kerry, Mary, Elizabeth, Martin

Robert Newton McIndoo

Geraldine Frances Quinn McIndoo

George Hugh Quinn (founding member of
Alcoholics Anonymous in Duluth, Minnesota)

Rose Rebecca Quinn

In acceptance there is peace.
In resistance there is pain.
The choice is always ours.
It is just that simple.
And no one ever said it was easy . . .
Peace, joy, and freedom lie in
realizing
the how, the process,
rather than the content of life.

—*The Key: And the Name of the Key Is Willingness*

Acknowledgments

I want to thank many people for their generous contributions to this book:

Judy Delaney and Caryn Pernu for their motive, inaugural support of my concept and writing.

Sid Farrar for his faith, trust, and integrity.

Pat Samples for her gentleness and sensitivity.

Judy Bemis and Amr Barrada for their message and spirit of Acceptance.

Stephen Mitchell for his translation of the *Tao te Ching*—a transformative influence in my life.

Doone Rowles (†1986), my grandmotherly childhood neighbor and surrogate mother, who acknowledged and honored my spirit and gifts, and in so doing, limited the severity of my own disorders-to-be.

My many friends who gave me (and continue to give me) emotional and spiritual support during the writing's extended period of concentration and attendant social withdrawal. In particular, I want to mention John A., John B., Karen, Paul, and my brothers Kerry and Marty.

Madeleine (woof) and Britten, McTaggart, and Doone (meow, meow, meow), who kept me company during the writing, waited for the lap or the walk, forgave my inattention, and who continue to remind me of what is truly important.

Introduction

This "meditation" book is different from other meditation books because recovery from co-occurring disorders is different. It needs awareness and acceptance of *two* problems—addiction as well as a mental health disorder—which are both similar and different, *inter*dependent and *in*dependent.

The Design of This Book

By reading this book regularly, you will learn about the process of recovery from co-occurring disorders, formerly referred to as a dual disorder. But it does not tell you what to do, it simply *shows* you what some mythical people may have done, or thought, in the course of a mythical year. You may also think of these entries as the diary of a composite person who is actively recovering from co-occurring disorders and has learned some things. The entries record this person's problems and pain as well as record the moments of insight or awareness, however limited, that make it possible to accept the problem and begin to deal with it. In a way, this book can be seen as a model, although the path it represents is only one of many paths to recovery. Thus, every entry will not apply to everyone's recovery—take what you like and leave the rest.

Though mythical, or composite, these feelings, experiences, and actions are based on those of real people in recovery from co-occurring disorders.

Clearly this meditation book differs from its cousins. It is written in the first-person "I" voice, essentially in the present tense. It tends to be simpler and shorter than other books, more educational, more direct, and more concrete.

Each entry, which has four parts, begins with the title, an affirmation in itself. The opening paragraph then identifies the pain or problem. The following paragraph explores some awareness or insight into it, arrived at through a combination of experience, memory, and the mysterious state of grace called "Aha!" The last paragraph, usually a single brief sentence, offers a simple and concrete action step—such as might be suggested by someone who cares about you and understands your problem and your process—one that will move you in the direction of recovery, no matter how small the step.

Why are the entries set up this way? Because awareness and acknowledgment bring about acceptance. Acceptance allows for action (or appropriate inaction). Appropriate action, no matter how small, results in change and growth. This is the nature of recovery.

Some Assumptions

While perhaps many in recovery can find support in this book, those with co-occurring disorders will feel more at home, will be most rewarded. You need a book that accepts and understands your particular struggles.

As a person in recovery from co-occurring disorders, chances are that

a. you are relatively new to recovery, whether from addiction or from a mental disorder;

b. you are becoming increasingly aware of your two disorders, regardless of which came first, which is more problematic, or which you're focusing on right now;

c. you are in some form of counseling or therapy (or are considering it);

d. you are taking a psychiatric medication (or might consider it);

e. you are working a Twelve Step program (or have some awareness of the Twelve Step fellowship, or are willing to participate in it); you are willing to apply its principles to recovery from both disorders;

f. you have a support person (or are willing to get one), whether in a Twelve Step fellowship (especially Dual Recovery Anonymous) or some other support program;

g. you have a plan for recovery (or are willing to develop one with the help of a counselor, therapist, or support person);

h. you are willing to reflect on your emotions and actions and make notes about what is going on in your life—since journaling yields greater insight than "thinking" alone. It also yields a written record that can reveal progress and problems.

Some Terms

Since the language of recovery may differ among treatment providers and kinds of recovery, here is a list of important words as they are used in this book.

Drugs usually means street drugs, but sometimes it includes alcohol (as in the phrase "alcohol and other drugs"). Drugs, however, *never* refers to (prescribed) medication.

High means intoxication by *either* street drugs or alcohol.

Cravings as used in addiction recovery, are considered a less immediate threat to abstinence or sobriety, and easier to deal with, than "urges." With urges, one is very close to having a slip.

Group refers to a Twelve Step group, a mental health support group, or other recovery group. Usually the kind of group is specified.

Symptoms is shorthand for mental health symptoms.

Meds is short for psychiatric medication.

Finally, although the Twelve Step fellowship uses the words "God" and "Higher Power," some people object to them. This book occasionally offers two substitutes, "helping power" and "source of power." Feel free, however, to use any words that work for you.

How to Use This Book

Although the style of this book is different, use it as you might use any other meditation book. Read entries according to the day of the month, regardless of where you are in recovery; check the index to find entries that speak to your day's concerns, for example, stigma, relapse, medication, or the Twelve Steps; or simply pick readings that appeal to you.

To Keep in Mind

The wellspring of this book is compassion. As you read it, please know that you are not alone, that there are people who can help, and that things will get better.

JANUARY

It helps if I do a little at a time.

When I realized I had an addiction, I felt guilty and defective. I wanted to shake off the problem right away. At first, I couldn't stay sober for long. I'd relapse and feel guilty and weak for having failed. I couldn't see that I was making progress.

Nowadays, I have a better perspective on the process—both on the downward and the upward spirals. I can see that it took some time for me to develop an addiction, one day at a time. And it took some time to feel so miserable that I really wanted to get clean. Likewise, it will take some time—one day at a time—to begin the changes that make for recovery. It's no fun to live with these problems, but I am slowly accepting the fact that change does not happen overnight. The most important thing I can do is to work at making some change each and every day.

Today I will do just one thing
to help my recovery progress.

I see how writing can help.

Typically, I don't like to write—I'm slow and self-conscious. I tend to worry too much about spelling and grammar and punctuation. I don't think I write well.

But I am learning now to write for myself as part of my recovery from co-occurring disorders. When I have an upsetting thought—or a helpful one—I write it down. This helps keep my mind clear and gives my fear and pain a place to go. By jotting down notes, I make a record of what I'm thinking and how I'm feeling. It helps me get to know myself better and helps me see my progress.

I will keep pen and paper handy, at home,
in the car, and at work.

I am doing the best I can.

I expected things to just fall into place once I accepted my problems, stopped using, and got into therapy. But that's not the case. Even though I'm abstinent now and going to weekly therapy and Twelve Step meetings, my mental health symptoms have gotten out of hand. Something is not working, or I'm doing something wrong.

But actually, that's not all bad. In the process of figuring out what led up to the relapse, I've learned another lesson in recovery: I can't change myself overnight, and willpower alone just doesn't work. I need to learn more about my co-occurring disorders, as well as how they affect myself and others. I need to learn ways to cope. If I accept myself and this subtle, slow process, I will recover, little by little, one day at a time.

I will write out an affirmation that reads:
"I am doing the right things. I am doing
the best I can."

I am no longer denying my feelings.

I used to use drugs all the time to forget my feelings—loneliness, anxiety, dread. Anytime I had strong or painful feelings, I promptly got high. In fact, I tried to make sure I was high much of the time, to make sure no painful feelings could creep in.

Now in recovery, I am changing. I am practicing living with my feelings—some of which I still don't want; many of which I didn't realize I had. Sometimes I still get overwhelmed. But in a way, I'm grateful for my emotions. As painful or frightening as they are at times, I am getting to know myself better, and I like who I am learning to see.

I will keep a "feelings log" today.
I'll jot down my strong feelings and
note any people involved.

I am learning to ask for help.

Some months before I finally got diagnosed (accurately) with co-occurring disorders, I knew I had a problem—maybe two problems. I could see that using alcohol and drugs wasn't helping my intense and disturbing moods. In fact, drinking and drug use were becoming a separate problem. Yet I was afraid (ashamed?) to talk to anyone. I couldn't ask for help, not for a long time.

Just by entering recovery, but especially by going to therapy and Twelve Step meetings, I've come to see that asking for help is a very good thing. It means I know something is wrong and that I can't fix it alone (Steps One and Two). Asking for help suggests that I'm willing to trust a power greater than myself (Step Three).

I will ask a recovering friend to call me tonight to ask me how I'm feeling.

I want my family to accept me.

When I first got sick, my family didn't know what was happening. They got angry. They implored, "What's wrong?" They said, "Straighten up!" They didn't know how difficult their demands were. They didn't know about addiction or mental disorders and that both need treatment and support. I think they were very afraid, for me and for themselves.

Of course, I didn't know the whole picture at first either. But through treatment, I am learning a lot about my disorders and about myself. I am slowly coming to accept both the way I am right now and my road to recovery. I believe that the more I accept myself, the more others will accept me.

I will pray for willingness to accept my family,
as they are, and ask my helpers to
bring us closer together.

*I am letting go of old friends
and making new ones.*

I didn't want to give up my old using friends. Most every day we would show up at the same place to keep each other company and get high. We trusted each other. We understood each other like nobody else (except others with mental disorders).

I still miss the old crowd and sometimes I want to visit them. But I don't. That would make it too easy to use again. I feel lonely at times, but I'm trying to let them go and slowly make new friends—sober and stable ones. Given the way I used to live my life, that's not easy. But there are a couple of people I can relate to these days. I will just have to give it some time.

*I will pray for the willingness to make friends;
I will pray for courage.*

If I take meds, I can't use drugs.

My psychiatrist said I needed to stop using all drugs and alcohol and take a psychiatric medication. She said that if I did, my symptoms would diminish. I wasn't sure if I believed her. Why should *her* medication take care of *my* symptoms better than *my* street drugs? I wanted to get better—and maybe medication could help—but I was afraid to give up my drugs.

Eventually, I got up the courage to tell all this to my support group. Several of them admitted that they were taking prescribed medication. They all agreed that it was tough to get clean and sober, but that medication acted on the body differently and really did work better than street drugs. Well, was I glad to hear this. It made it a lot easier for me to believe my doctor, get clean, and give medication a try.

*I will ask my support group and my
doctor to help me get abstinent
and then stay stable.*

*I better accept myself when
I am able to accept others.*

Even though I'm working a program of recovery for my addiction and a mental health disorder, I'm still having some disturbing symptoms and I can't go back to my old job yet. At times, I find myself withdrawing; at times, I feel bad because my recovery is not where I want it to be.

Fortunately, I tend to feel better about myself when I go to a support group meeting. My fellow members have problems much like mine. They, too, are working a program for co-occurring disorders, and they are recovering. What I find is that as I accept them, I am more willing to accept myself.

*I will schedule two support group meetings
each week as part of my recovery plan.*

*I will give the Twelve Step
fellowship a fair chance.*

I went to a Twelve Step meeting—as my counselor
suggested—and I didn't like it. It felt so different from
my support group. The meeting seemed formal, and I
felt uneasy when people talked about God and a "Higher
Power."

On the other hand, maybe I overreacted. I know I
don't like doing new things. I know I'm not eager to face
my problem with drug use these days. To tell the truth,
I did hear some helpful comments about being willing
and staying abstinent. Maybe I need to follow the facil-
itator's suggestion—take what I like and leave the rest.
Maybe I could get some help there after all. (And if this
meeting doesn't work out, there are other Twelve Step
meetings to try.)

*As suggested for newcomers,
I will give my Twelve Step meeting
five more chances.*

I am not helpless.

When I read about Step One, I realize that although I am powerless over my addiction, I am not powerless over my recovery. My addiction is stronger than I am alone, but I can still do something about it.

I have worked hard to get this far in recovery. Not only do I *not* feel helpless or victimized any longer, I feel stronger than ever before. Through Twelve Step and support meetings, therapy, and temporary medication, I am taking good care of myself. I don't have control over my co-occurring disorders, but I do have some tools now—along with growing faith in myself and strength.

> *I will pray the Serenity Prayer and take*
> *five minutes to think about the things*
> *I can—and cannot—change.*

I need to think twice about using.

I can't stop thinking and I can't sit still. I'm tired of TV and radio and social media. The next appointment with my counselor is two days away. Right now I don't much care what he said about mixing alcohol with meds. I can't stand the way I'm feeling. I have to relax. I want a drink.

But if I have one drink, I'll probably have another. If I have two, I'll have a dozen. I might wake up in detox again. I might have a setback. Maybe a drink isn't the best thing for me after all.

When I have strong cravings, I will stop
whatever I'm doing for two minutes
and think about my options.

I am learning about "good" drugs.

For a long time, I thought a "good" drug was one that was strong, cheap, and easy to get. It was a very "good" drug if it got me high fast and kept me high for a long time.

Now, in recovery, I see drugs differently. I am learning that a good drug is prescribed for me by a doctor (especially a psychiatrist who knows addiction and recovery) and purchased at a pharmacy. A good drug helps me cope with my mental disorder; it does not get me high. Such a drug is best called a *medication*. Unlike when I take street drugs, if I have any problems with my medication, I can call my doctor for assistance.

At my next recovery meeting I will share my old and new understanding of "good" drugs.

I am grateful for my abstinence.

It's scary to remember what life was like when I was still using. Only now can I see how much I was acting out, how out of control I was, and how afraid I was of facing my problems.

Once I got clean and sober, I could hold my head up again. I knew better where I was at, and my psychiatrist could diagnose the somewhat hidden problem in my life—a mental disorder. And because I was abstinent, I had more strength to face this new challenge in what has become my recovery from co-occurring disorders.

I will write out two ways abstinence
has helped me in recovering from
my mental disorder.

I don't have to blame myself.

I know myself enough to know that when I make a mistake, even a small one, I can be hard on myself. With co-occurring disorders, I am more apt to make mistakes and so am more vulnerable than ever. All too often I feel shameful, guilty, defective. I'm scared by how much I dislike myself at times.

Fortunately, my therapist has helped me deal with these strong feelings. I am learning that (*a*) I am not to blame for my disorders; they are caused by numerous factors—biological, psychological, and social—none of which I'm responsible for. (*b*) I *am* responsible for my recovery. (*c*) Making mistakes is not a bad thing. Mistakes are one of my many teachers. (*d*) The more I accept this, the easier it is for me to accept my situation and take my struggle in stride.

I will look at a recent mistake to see
what I can learn from it.

I am making changes.

When I woke up this morning, I wanted to pull the sheets over my head and go back to sleep—restless sleep crowned with a nightmare. Yet what hit me harder were my unresolved problems—the ones I fell asleep worrying about last night.

But instead of going back to sleep (instead of doing the first thing that came to mind like I used to do), I sat up in bed and called my support person. I told her how worried I was, how I really wanted to go back to sleep, but how I had enough resolve to make a call. We talked a little while and sure enough, I felt better—especially when I realized that *I had done something new.* With that boost, I promptly got up, got dressed, and ate breakfast.

I will take a risk today and try one new approach with an ongoing problem.

Medication is part of my recovery.

I am grateful that both of my long-term disorders are now in remission. Still, I need daily medication for my mental disorder, and that makes me feel ashamed. I feel like there's something deeply wrong with me, something that separates me, painfully, from others. It hurts.

When I mentioned this feeling to my therapist, she helped. She explained to me that taking medication is like wearing prescription eyeglasses. It's uncomfortable at first, but after a while, it will become a more natural part of my life. Medication will let me see clearly where I am and what I need to do in recovery.

*I will talk with my support group
about the stigma I feel and the
strength of my recovery.*

I need to be aware of my symptoms.

I need to be aware of my mental health symptoms (I've certainly had them often enough). For example, I start to feel irritable, drive too fast, and spend more money than I can afford. In a few days, I'm staying up all night reading or cleaning or writing long letters to people I hardly know.

Until recently, I couldn't see what was happening to me (in fact, a manic phase) until I was looking up from the bottom of a well (a depressed phase). Of course, by then it was too late. But now that I am learning more about my disorders, I believe I'll be able to see the warning signs sooner and prevent a relapse.

I will keep a log of thoughts and feelings
that usually precede a psychiatric episode.

I want more freedom.

My co-occurring disorders have cost me some freedom. Life now feels complicated and cluttered. I have to take meds regularly (not to mention go for med checks), attend treatment several times a week, and go to my Twelve Step meeting once a week. At times my disability feels like a cage.

While it's true that recovery takes time, attention, and energy, it takes no more than my addiction did. The more I accept my disorders and make recovery a regular part of my day, the more I can recover. And the more I recover, the more stable and self-reliant I can become, using my new strengths and coping skills. I am reclaiming my life as I rebuild it, one day at a time.

I will carefully follow the activities on today's recovery plan—my path to freedom.

I am responsible for my recovery.

Some days I want to blame my mental disorder on my addiction. Some days I want to blame my addiction on my mental disorder. Or I could blame them both on my genes or my parents. In short, I don't want to face these problems. (Who would?)

What I am learning, however, is that although I am not to blame for having co-occurring disorders (each disorder is a no-fault disorder), I *am* responsible for my recovery. No one can take these problems away. They are, indeed, mine. And as much as I wish it weren't so, I am the one who must deal with them (with lots of support).

With the help of my doctor, therapist,
or sponsor (or all three), I will develop
a formal recovery plan.

I can handle the panicky feelings.

I know the frightening feeling; I know instantly that something's wrong. Suddenly I feel hot, dizzy, then chilled. My heart beats fast and hard, and I can't catch my breath. I'm caught off guard and can hardly move. I think I'm going to die.

Funny thing. I don't die. The worst has never happened. Every time I've had a panic attack, I've managed to catch my breath and get to a place of safety. No passing out, no heart attack. It's hard for me to believe sometimes, but my Higher Power is taking care of me. I continue to muddle through, and I am grateful.

I will think up a brief prayer or affirmation
to help me feel safe when I feel panicky.

I am learning to let go.

I had dreams for my life. I envisioned that one day, I would have a family and a house and a good job. I dreamed my dream for a happy life. I never dreamed I would develop co-occurring disorders and perhaps have to let go of some dreams.

But in coming as far as I have in my recovery, I now believe that I have a Higher Power who truly cares about me and wants me to be happy. And I am learning to trust my Higher Power. I believe that I can still have a happy life, although it may look different from the vision in my dreams.

I will read Step Three and pray
to accept myself and my life.

I want to become more open.

When I joined a recovery group, I knew the purpose was to talk more about my problems, and I knew it would help. Unfortunately, but understandably, at first I could not. I was too shy to admit how I behaved when drinking and afraid to admit how I felt when I had my mental health symptoms. I was afraid I'd be rejected and then feel even worse.

I am glad to say that my assumption was incorrect. Group members were typically nonjudgmental, and when I felt strong enough to share my story, I was fully supported—even encouraged. Moreover, once I'd opened up to my group, I felt less vulnerable, more accepted, more at peace. My risk earned an unexpected reward.

At my next meeting I will share a little about myself and see how it feels.

I can pray for my needs.

In part, I am afraid to pray. If I get what I ask for, I may feel guilty, as if I don't deserve it. If my request is not met, I may feel rejected, angry, unworthy.

But slowly I am learning that it's OK to have needs, and that to get my needs met I must ask for help at times. I am learning that a "no" does not mean I'm a bad person or that I am unworthy. My Higher Power is accepting and forgiving and will not reject me.

Today I will talk with my sponsor and a friend
about the Eleventh Step and prayer.

I need to accept the help professionals can give me.

I never liked doctors. I hate being sick. I resent the loss of control and feeling so vulnerable.

Well, I'm sick again. I have an addiction and a mental health disorder. And I am faced with not just a doctor, but with counselors, therapists, case managers, and social workers. I don't want to be sick, to lose control, to need help. But after long denying my disorders and struggling on my own, I can see that I need professional help. I wouldn't be here if I could have done it on my own.

I will read about Step Two today and
pray for the willingness to trust.

I need to get out more.

I feel shaky and fragile these days. I've been sad and quiet for so long—eating alone, working alone, being alone with my thoughts. It hurts and it's hard to face the world.

On the other hand, maybe it hurts *because* I'm withdrawing, *because* I'm not facing the world. Perhaps I could call a friend to talk with or walk with; perhaps I could go to a coffee shop or to the zoo. (Of course, I could always go to a Twelve Step or support group meeting.) Although I don't feel like taking action now, perhaps now is the best time to do something to help my mood. It will help if I can move toward the world instead of away from it.

Today I will try one new activity
that involves other people.

I am willing to get help.

I was afraid to ask for help at first, because I was afraid to learn that I was indeed sick. Then I was afraid that my employer and friends would find out. I couldn't accept having an addiction and a mental disorder. In the meantime, my problems kept getting worse.

But now that I have managed to begin my recovery, I can see that to be willing to ask for help, I first had to hit bottom. I had to believe that it would be more painful *not* to change. Today I attend treatment and my Twelve Step group twice a week. I am doing the best I can, and I am getting better—with help.

I will practice trusting my helpers
and pray for courage to continue
my recovery.

I am grateful for my life.

Yes, there's been much pain in my life. I have had extreme ups and downs. Yes, I have lived with addiction and with serious emotional problems. I have even been suicidal. These problems have cost me spiritually, emotionally, and physically. But I still have life, *my* life, and I am grateful.

In recovery from co-occurring disorders I can see that I am not done realizing my potential. I still have the chance to change and grow. With the help of my Higher Power, I am developing the necessary acceptance, strength, and courage. Recovery shows me how I can integrate my experience to make today better.

I will say a prayer today
in gratitude for my life.

I am learning about patience and rest.

At night I have trouble falling asleep. During the day I have racing, tumbling thoughts. The medication for my mental health disorder isn't helping as much as I had hoped. I feel tired much of the time.

Fortunately, my doctor is supportive. He reassures me that many people feel this way as they begin to recover from addiction and mental disorder. He says that once the medication is at full strength, my thinking will get clearer and sleep will come easier. I'm glad I can trust my doctor. I will give this more time to begin resolving.

I will take some quiet time during the day
and go to sleep early tonight.

I need to take care of myself.

It's hard for me to do Step Eight and recall the names of people I have harmed. I don't want to think about them or what I've done—especially what I've done to one person: myself.

I need to put myself on my Step Eight list. Given my co-occurring disorders, I believe it will help if I see how I've failed to take care of myself (or perhaps even been self-destructive). When I think about this, I feel sad. Because in recovery, I am learning that I am worthy of better. I look forward to making a change.

I will write my name in my journal and then
list two ways I've harmed myself and two ways
I'm now taking care of myself.

I need to monitor my symptoms.

I get less and less interested in work and what I eat. I feel run down, almost ill, and can't seem to get going. Sometimes I can't think straight, sometimes I can't stop thinking, and sometimes all my thoughts are gloomy.

For me, the clue that I'm giving in to depression is gloomy thoughts. Odd as it is, I want to keep thinking them. They're comforting somehow (because they're familiar?) and yet very painful. But in recovery, I can see that this symptom, among the others, is a warning sign and that I need to give it prompt attention.

When my thoughts are too dark or when dark thoughts persist, I will stay in touch with a trusted friend or my counselor.

FEBRUARY

I can find a silver lining.

Of course, if given a choice, I would never have asked for co-occurring disorders—two disorders that affect one another and require an extended period of recovery. But here I am—and here they are—like it or not!

And yet I can see now that *because of* hitting bottom, *because of* the pain and suffering, I have found a new faith and a better way to live. In my process of recovery, I have found my Higher Power. While "spirituality" used to seem like a foreign word, *becoming spiritual* is now an integral part of my life.

> *I will take five minutes today to think*
> *of one improvement in my life that has*
> *come about through my disorders.*

I will be taken care of.

I used to wonder if anyone was listening to my prayers for help with my disorders—the mood swings and the drug use. I felt alone and out of control. I felt as if no one cared and eventually wondered if I was worth caring about.

And yet looking back at that time—not so long ago—I wonder if perhaps I was the one who lost faith in myself, who stopped caring about myself. Because once I chose *recovery*, once I chose recovery *for myself*, I began to experience the care and love of many people—in treatment, in the clinic, and in my recovery groups. These days I know that I am worthy, I believe my prayers and requests for help are being heard, and I trust that I will be taken care of.

I will take five minutes today to remember
the people who have been helping me
in my recovery.

I still want to feel my emotions.

For a while it hurt so bad that I couldn't stand it anymore—anger, then rage, abandonment, crying myself to sleep, then emptiness. Yet now that I'm finally on medication I feel almost nothing. It's as though the switch to my emotions were shut off. I'm numb.

Medication is a therapy I now know I need for my mental health disorder. But if I am overmedicated, flattened out, I have no emotions to work on and it's hard to care about anything. As painful as it has been, I do not want to feel numb. I still want to feel my emotions, even if some of them still hurt.

I will call my doctor promptly, explain what's
going on, and ask about an adjustment
in my medication.

*I need a group that accepts
my co-occurring disorders.*

I wonder if I should have let my Step group know that I
also have a mental disorder. It didn't go well—they got
so quiet and looked away. I doubt they would ever have
known the difference. I only mentioned it because I was
trying to be honest, as I've learned to be in recovering
from addiction.

Right now I feel hurt and misunderstood. I even feel
rejected, ashamed. But why should *I* be rejected? All of
us in the meeting are addicts. It's just that some of us are
tall, some short; some black, some white; some men,
some women. And some of us—I suspect more than
one of us—have a mental health disorder in addition to
addiction. We are all more alike than different.

*If needed, I will contact Central Service or my
local Intergroup to find a Twelve Step group
that fully accepts my two disorders.*

I can write down my thoughts and feelings.

These days I'm afraid I'm not thinking clearly (although the medication I'm taking helps). I'm not remembering things all that well either. There's much on my mind and I have many problems to deal with.

In my Twelve Step meeting, I noticed a friend carrying a daily journal. I asked him about it and he quickly recommended it. He says he uses his journal to write down his thoughts and feelings a few times each day. He says it helps him understand better what's going on with him. Well, I'm no writer—and I'm not sure what I'd say in a journal—but I can see how such a tool might help me see things more clearly too. It's worth a try.

I will take five minutes in the morning
and five minutes in the evening to
record some of my thoughts.

I need a sponsor.

Sometimes my attitude doesn't help; sometimes my attitude even hurts. I want to do things on my own, in my own way, and in my own time. I don't much like authority or rules. I have a strong will. Yet thinking and behaving based solely on this attitude is part of my addiction.

Now that I've taken Step One and admitted I can't do this alone, it's clear to me that I need the help of a support person, someone to prevent me from being my own worst enemy. I don't want my resistance and fears to lead me astray or hold me back. I need a guide, a coach, someone who has already walked a mile (or two) in my shoes.

> *At my next Twelve Step meeting I will take*
> *the first step. I will look for someone*
> *to be my temporary sponsor.*

*I can admit that I have addiction
and a mental health disorder.*

At times before recovery, I was losing control over my moods and over my life. I felt like I was coming apart. One week I felt on top of the world; the next month I was in the gutter. It didn't help that I kept drinking through it all. I was afraid, I was in danger, and I didn't know where to turn.

I threatened suicide—spent two nights in a locked ward—and got a clue. At rock bottom, I realized there was only one way left to go. First, I admitted to myself that I no longer had control over my life. Then I admitted this fact to another person: I asked for help. In doing so, I had taken the First Step.

*I will humbly share my Step One story
and talk about the relief, freedom, and
strength of admitting (and accepting)
my co-occurring disorders.*

I am building a new source of strength.

When I had symptoms of my mental health disorder, I used street drugs to manage them. Drugs were my Higher Power. They seemed to do what I thought I couldn't do. When I used them, I seemed to feel better— briefly. But instead of restoring my mental and emotional health, the drugs led to addiction, and the addiction has made my mental health recovery that much harder. Now I must work on two disorders together.

These days, it's clear that I won't find relief in street drugs. Real relief comes from people, caring people who accept and understand my no-fault disorders. With the help of my friends and others in recovery from co-occurring disorders, I can remain both stable and sober.

I will make a commitment to myself to spend more time with people who have the experience, strength, and hope that can help me recover.

I want to face my liabilities.

I've been afraid to do Steps Four and Five. Although it makes sense to become more honest about myself, I'm afraid of the guilt and the shame—some of which I'm feeling already. I am afraid that somehow I'll be rejected or punished. Yet what I need more than anything is understanding and acceptance.

As I have struggled (and watched others struggle) with these two Steps, I've learned that their acceptance and forgiveness are so important to my recovery. But I've also learned that one must be ready to do them. (There is no hurry. There are no tests. And it's OK to take my time.) Before working on Steps Four and Five, I need faith in my Higher Power, trust in the program, and the courage to face my liabilities.

> *When I feel ready, first I will carefully pace*
> *my inventory. Then I'll select a Fifth Step*
> *listener who truly understands recovery*
> *from co-occurring disorders.*

I can get by with less money.

Recovering from two chronic disorders costs money. And these days I have little—all I can manage is a part-time job. Sometimes it's hard to pay the bills. I miss what extra money I used to have. I can't have fun the way I used to.

On the other hand, does that mean I can't have any fun at all? In the Sunday paper I noticed a list of free events for "folks on a budget" (that's me—and apparently I'm not alone!). True, money is important, but maybe I don't have to let it be *so* important. Maybe this is a chance for me to change how I think about money.

I will make a note of two free things I like to do, or two free places I like to go, and tack the note on my bulletin board.

I help myself when I help others.

Some nights when the phone rings, I hope it isn't a friend calling for support. Even though I have some time in recovery, I've still got my own worries. I've still got my own pain. Some nights I just don't have the energy for helping.

And yet, somewhere, through my Higher Power, I find the energy. When I hear a voice in pain, when I am asked for help, I know that I can listen. I don't have to take on the pain or fix the problem, but I can be a good listener. And when the conversation is over, I can feel lighter about my own worries and yet stronger for having helped.

I will answer any call for support with
all the strength of my program.

It is an honor to be supportive.

It's an honor (and a gift) when a friend calls for support. As I listen, I am reminded of my own stages of recovery—what I've felt, experienced, learned.

And when I listen deeply—when I am fully present—I can see myself in the speaker and realize that I, too, have more to learn. I have come to see that recovery is discovery—a wondrous experience of becoming open to whatever life brings.

I will welcome and respect any call
for support as a chance to learn more
about recovery—as a "teacher."

I want to deal with my painful emotions.

I feel alone, lost, and afraid. Again. Once again, I find myself thinking about escaping from my sadness and anger by getting high or drunk. Yet I would only plunge myself into more guilt, shame, and remorse. Instead of producing relief, it would produce a lapse.

I don't want to do this again. It hurts too much and helps too little. But the good news is that I am slowly, *truly,* learning that using drugs and alcohol doesn't prevent emotions—it only postpones them. It keeps me from facing them and then adds a new layer of painful emotions. I am looking forward to change.

When I need to release pain, I will try writing about it, drawing it, or talking about it with a friend, sponsor, or therapist.

I can be forgiven.

As I look closely at my assets and liabilities in Step Four, I see mistakes I am not proud of. I see mistakes that I still feel guilty about. It hurts to realize that I cannot undo them. It hurts even to admit them.

Yet in my recovery program, there is forgiveness. The more meetings I attend and the more I share, the more I sense the love and care of my fellow members. And the more they accept me and where I am in recovery—with my faults, failings, and problems—the more I accept myself, and the less shameful and guilty I feel. In the fellowship, I experience true forgiveness.

> *I will forgive one mistake I make today*
> *and one mistake of another.*

It will help if I let go.

When will this roller-coaster ride stop? I work my recovery program for my addiction and mental health disorder and *still* I have setbacks. I feel stuck. What else can I possibly do to get better? Sometimes I feel helpless. On very bad days, I feel hopeless.

And yet, when I take a deep breath and look back at the first three Steps, my program reminds me (yet again) that I do not control my disorders. My program reminds me of my Higher Power, who will help me cope with my struggles, who will help me recover, if I allow it. If I allow it, if I turn my will and my life over, I will know what to do to avoid the slips, prevent the setbacks, and regain stability. If I let that power help, I will get better.

I will review Steps One, Two, and
Three and pray for courage.

I now know I need people.

I've been thinking about how nervous I feel around people. I have co-occurring disorders and I feel different from them. In part, I'm afraid of having symptoms when others are present. Sometimes I feel embarrassed. Sometimes I'm too afraid to talk.

And then it dawned on me that, nowadays, even though my disorders make it harder for me to be with people, I'm not willing to feel alone anymore. Deep down I crave companionship, friendship. *I need people.* These days in particular, I need the experience, strength, and hope of my fellow Twelve Steppers.

At my recovery meeting I will arrive early to help set up (or take a turn at being a greeter).

I have found the help I needed.

Before getting into recovery, I had little faith and trusted no one (not even myself). I was trying (and failing) to manage two difficult disorders on my own. Basically, I used drugs to change my mood and I kept my problems to myself. Finally (predictably), I hit bottom. Finally, I realized how much I needed help.

And I have found help in the Twelve Step fellowship. When I go to my recovery meeting, I feel connected; I learn that people will be there for me. When I meet with my sponsor, I feel reassured. I learn that it's OK to have these problems. I also learn that it's good to talk about them (because that's how they get better). Getting help when I need it makes it easier for me to believe that I, too, have a Higher Power, one who is quietly and subtly helping me recover. Finally, I am learning trust, and my spirit is growing stronger.

I will meditate on two things
that help me feel taken care of,
that help me feel secure.

I am preparing to make amends.

It is hard for me to think about facing the people I've harmed through my addiction. I imagine that I will suddenly lose the strength to tell them I'm sorry, to tell them I want to make amends. I am afraid they won't accept me or my offer.

Yet I must try. Because in listening to my fellow members talk about the Steps, I am learning how important it is to be free of the past. I see how releasing myself from guilt is critical to staying sober and stable. I am glad that I have taken my time in working the first eight Steps, because to do Step Nine, I will need all the courage (and all the humility) I can muster.

When I feel strong enough in my recovery, I will ask my sponsor for extra support as I begin to make amends to people I have harmed.

I have some liabilities and weaknesses.

I am valuable and lovable. I have much to offer. But as a person in recovery from addiction and a mental disorder, I am figuring out that some aspects of my personality need work.

To learn which parts need work, I must examine how I think and how I behave. It will help if I take a careful look at how I make it harder for myself to recover—that is, if I look at my liabilities and weaknesses. It is not easy or pleasant to face these parts of me, let alone consider changing them. But recovery—in other words, slowly making changes in my life—is the most important work I need to do right now.

I will write down two ways I think or two ways
I behave that can make it harder for me
to stay in recovery.

I continue to benefit from treatment.

I couldn't stop worrying. I couldn't relax. I could hardly get out of the house at times. I was stuck in a pattern, feeling anxious and fearful, and using alcohol to feel better (although it was not much help).

But what did help me to get unstuck and feel better was going through treatment. Once I learned about my two disorders—a mental health disorder and a substance use disorder—my anxiety diminished, and I was able to stop using alcohol. These days I am starting to do things differently and to do different things. I even take a (healthy) risk now and then. The freedom of choice is a great relief.

I will meditate on the changes in my life
and the expanding options that have
come about through treatment.

I need time to change.

Getting into recovery, it was hard enough to admit my mental health disorder and my addiction. For some time after, I could hardly *see* my character defects, let alone admit to them.

Having done a Fourth, Fifth, and Sixth Step, I feel willing—no, eager—to let go of my shortcomings. But as much as I want to change now, I can't just say "Change!" and be changed. My addiction has taught me that change requires time, patience, and the help of my Higher Power. As I continue to work the program, I need to be aware of my shortcomings and allow them to be removed by my Higher Power when the time is right.

Today I will pray for patience
and self-acceptance.

I am doing well.

For a while, the pain of my co-occurring disorders was so great, I could hardly believe I would ever be OK again. I had little strength and saw no way out. Yet in detox one day, a miracle happened: I finally hit bottom.

These days I take a walk around the block twice a day, sometimes with a friend from my support group. Recently I met with my sponsor, and she'll be giving me my anniversary pin next week. With my doctor's help I am now taking a medication that diminishes the symptoms from my mental health disorder with even fewer side effects. Looking back, I am amazed—amazed and grateful. Because today, I am sober and stable.

I will strengthen my commitment
to recovery by offering to do service
at my Twelve Step meeting.

I don't have to believe in God
to have a Higher Power.

When I first tried the Twelve Step program, I thought I had to believe in God to recover from my disorders. I thought maybe it was a religious organization, and I wanted no part of it. This made it harder for me to attend six trial meetings, as my therapist had suggested.

But somehow—my Higher Power perhaps?—I stuck with it, and I have since learned differently. I've learned that to recover, all I need to do is believe two things: that I cannot recover on my own and that something else can help me. For instance, some people consider the group itself a Higher Power and some use a friend or sponsor. Knowing this, I can work Step Two and continue in my spiritual recovery.

I will draw a picture or write a brief
description of my Higher Power.

I have a simple job to do.

I suppose it's not unusual, but my life is highly troubled at this stage of my recovery. I am going through many changes and feeling much pain. When I hit bottom a while back, I thought my problems were at their worst. But these days, they seem little better. I feel frustrated and confused.

So I took my struggles to my Step group and, as usual, got some support. I was reminded that it will help if I keep my life, my focus, as simple as possible these days. I have only one task with two parts: stay abstinent and stable. Nothing is more important. If I take Step One, accept that I have these problems, and keep coming to meetings so I can get support working the rest of the program, I will recover. It's that simple.

I will make a reminder card that reads
"Today I want abstinence and stability.
I will do what it takes to recover."

I can pray again.

I used to dislike praying. Out of anger and fear, I could hardly imagine a Higher Power. I was afraid of prayer's silence, afraid to be alone with my thoughts and feelings. Prayer seemed mysterious and tied up with religion. I don't think I believed in it.

In recovery, all this has changed. I see my Higher Power as accepting and caring. The fear of silence and solitude has been lifted. Slowly, through doubting and testing, I have come to believe in prayer. It is simple, personal, and powerful. For my return to prayer, I am grateful.

I will set a time and talk with
my Higher Power today.

I can manage my anxiety and my addiction.

My anxiety disorder kept getting worse. It got harder to go to the grocery store and harder even to drive my car. Eventually, I couldn't leave my apartment, and then I lost my job. To solve my mental health problem, I tried street drugs and alcohol. They didn't help at all; in fact, I developed co-occurring disorders.

Given both my addiction *and* the mental disorder, I learned to work a recovery program for co-occurring disorders. For me, this means I use the Twelve Steps for both disorders. It means that I see a therapist regularly and attend an anxiety support group every week. Through the help of my combined recovery program and my Higher Power, I now have my anxiety in check and I am gratefully abstinent from alcohol or other drugs.

I will meditate on the advantages
of using specific recovery programs
for my specific disorders.

I am working on trust.

When I read Step Three and think about turning my will and life over to the care of a Higher Power, I don't want to do it. Since it is hard for me to trust anyone at all, it doesn't make sense to trust something I can't see and haven't met. It is even harder when I recall friends I thought I could trust but who let me down.

And yet, even though I'm afraid to trust, I realize that I actually do it every day. What about that ride in my friend's car? I trusted *her*. What about that plane trip I took? I never saw the pilot, but I trusted *him*. And what about the ride in the taxi? (Never mind!) Or how did I know what was *really* in the medication I picked up from my pharmacist? Of course, I didn't know. I just *trusted her*—like all the others—and it's worked!

> *I will write down the names of two people*
> *or things I don't trust these days, and then*
> *two people or things I do trust.*

I have friends to help me.

I am having strong mental health symptoms these days. My doctor has given me a new medication to help manage them. Unfortunately, it has some side effects that could affect my driving. So I won't be driving my car for a while, at least until my symptoms get under better control and I adjust to the medication.

Being without a car—well, here's another loss of freedom. It's tough living with co-occurring disorders—two disorders that regularly affect my life. But I managed before without a car (after three DUIs and losing my driver's license). With the help of my Higher Power, I will manage again.

I will tell my friends about my transportation problem and ask them for help.

I look forward to my meeting.

I now know I *need* contact with people and I *want* to be with people at times. But having co-occurring disorders makes it hard. Without alcohol or other drugs (my former crutch), I often feel shy and uncomfortable around people. Still, I want to be accepted *as a person*, regardless of my disorders.

At my meeting, acceptance is exactly what I get. Week in and week out, I share a part of my life, say what's working and what's not, and offer whatever strength I have. In return I get respect and caring, as well as spiritual and emotional support. This is a gift. I did not know such benefits were possible. I feel humble and immensely grateful.

I will put together a schedule of Twelve Step meetings (such as Dual Recovery Anonymous and other Twelve Step groups) and keep it handy.

MARCH

I feel lighter and stronger.

When I was still using—and even after several months of abstinence—it seemed that much in my life was a struggle. Some days it took all I had to get through the day (or the hour). I didn't think I could do it.

But I held on (I guess I had faith). And these days I find myself feeling lighter. The obsession has truly been lifted, and my emotional problems are manageable. I feel less vulnerable. I feel stronger in my program. I do not feel the fear as before. These days I feel more alive than I can scarcely remember. I sense that I can do what I need to do for my recovery. Slowly, the promises that follow Step Nine are coming true.

Today I will thank my Higher Power
for my progress and pray for deeper
acceptance of my life.

I wonder about quitting my medication.

I write squiggly because my hand shakes. I feel edgy much of the time. Even my digestion is out of sync. I don't feel like keeping up with my medication schedule with these side effects.

On the other hand, I know I need this medication for my mental health disorder. I felt horrible, helpless, and hopeless before it started working. If I stop taking it now, I might get seriously ill again. I want to stay stable. I want to keep working my recovery program. I just may have to cope with these secondary problems for now.

I will call my psychiatrist to report
any problems with my medication and
ask for reassurance and support.

I feel good when I share at meetings.

Even though I can't always put into words just what I have in mind, I am now sharing at my meetings and my fellow members are listening to me. I realize how good it feels to say what I'm feeling and be known.

I have been shy and reserved much of my life, but in treatment eventually I got used to seeing a circle of people looking at me. And it got easier to think on my feet. Now at my regular Twelve Step meeting, I like it when they pay attention to me. I feel like a part of the group. I feel especially good when someone thanks me for sharing.

I will write down two other ways I can become a stronger part of my recovery group.

I don't have to be alone with the pain.

These days, I'm not sleeping well and I'm tired most of the time. I'm OK at work for a while, but then I can't stop the memories and I can't concentrate. At times I feel disconnected from the world. Some days I have to leave work and go home, where I feel guilty and alone with my disorders. It's hard not to think about using.

But it may not have to get so bad (and it doesn't have to get any worse). When I manage to pause for a moment and take a deep breath, I realize I can call my sponsor and support person, my first lines of help. I can call them at work or at home. When I talk, they listen closely (even when I cry). I am grateful for their support. They care about me. I trust them—and need to let them help me more.

I will put together a list of my supportive friends and their telephone numbers.

I can't use alcohol or other drugs
when I take medication.

I want to feel better. My symptoms are tormenting me. My doctor told me it would take a couple of weeks for my medication to work, but it's been longer than that now and I feel like I can't hold on. Today, I'd just as soon score some of my *own* drugs again. I *know* I'd feel better—right away—if I took *them*.

And yet, I also know that if I mixed street drugs with my medication, I could get very sick. I would lose my sobriety. And I would be taking back the control I gave to my Higher Power in Step Three.

I will pray to my Higher Power for the
courage and strength to resist the urges
and to find healthy ways to cope.

I am learning how to break my patterns.

Sometimes a less healthy voice in me still runs through the old lines: *If I drink enough, I can stop my troubling thoughts. I'll have a hangover the next day, but at least the thoughts will be gone for a while. I don't like being hungover, but I can't stand feeling so trapped inside my head.*

In the midst of an episode with my co-occurring disorders, it's hard to hear the voice of my Higher Power. But on a day like today, when I'm thinking clearly, I hear healthy messages like these: *Be sure to take your medication faithfully. Try a relaxation exercise. Call a friend and go for a walk. But whatever you do, don't drink—it makes things worse in the long run.*

> *I will write down two steps I can take*
> *to help me avoid using when I'm*
> *having symptoms.*

I can ask for help.

One thing I don't like about recovery from my co-occurring disorders is having to ask for help. (Normally, I wouldn't borrow a dime from a friend.) When I need help, sometimes I feel ashamed and vulnerable. When I ask for help, sometimes I feel like I'm causing trouble and I'm afraid I'll be rejected.

As I talked about this issue with my co-occurring recovery support group, I was reminded of two things: (*a*) I'm a person who is worthy of help. (*b*) I have two biological disorders that need treatment and follow-up care—just like heart disease or a broken bone. If I can keep these awarenesses in mind, I can learn to deal with the loss of control—and freedom—that come with needing help.

> *I will write out a card that reads*
> *"It's OK to ask for help. It means*
> *I'm taking care of myself."*

I want to feel useful and productive.

For a while I hardly knew who I was or where I was. But slowly, with medication and a good therapy group, I got reoriented and back on my feet. Now I'm sober and stable, and I feel much stronger.

I don't want to just hang around anymore. I want to use my talents to make something, or make something work. I want to help. I want to be with other people these days. In fact, I'm ready to go back to work. I believe I can handle it now. I want to earn my keep again.

I will talk with professionals who can help me with getting a part-time job and vocational training.

I have one goal today: stay clean and sober.

I want to do it. I know I can do it. I've done it before. I will do it again. Now that my mental health symptoms are getting better, I want to stop using more than anything else. I want my life back again—all of it.

Today I know what to do and I know who can help me. I have no excuses anymore. I'll be OK without my drug. The most important thing in my life today is staying straight. Today it's the *only* thing I have to do.

*I will write out the most important thing
I can do to remain abstinent on this
clean-and-sober day.*

I don't have to stay depressed all day.

This morning I woke up again from a nightmare (not fun!). I'm not surprised—they've been showing up now and then as I deal with this depression. At first I felt so bad I didn't think I could get out of bed—but somehow, I did. And then, somehow, I showered, ate, and took my medication. Somehow, I completed my early morning routine.

I'm surprised by my strength (and pleased). This afternoon I feel better; in fact, I feel pretty good right now. I don't feel tired or sad or guilty. I think I feel good enough to walk around the park. This change feels great.

I will spend five minutes today thinking about how a recovery plan helps me stay abstinent and stable.

I can take the time I need to recover.

I tend to want things when I want them, and usually that means *now*. I want to be recovered *now*. I want to feel whole and healthy *now*. I am impulsive and impatient.

But my Twelve Step program is teaching me the truer meaning of *now*: with the help of my Higher Power, I accept where I'm at in my recovery. To me this means I know I can't just say "*Be well*" and then be well. Change is slow and methodical. To recover, I need to take small steps every day. I must work on each problematic symptom, habit, routine, thought pattern, or attitude *one at a time and one day at a time.*

> *Following my Step Ten inventory, I will select something I want to change and work on changing it today.*

When I "think bad," I feel bad.

I just realized how much I've been silently talking to myself. I'm surprised at how negative this self-talk is. I've been hearing self-defeating thoughts such as I'm so alone and I'm never going to get well. I can see how these thoughts could keep me down.

Maybe this is what my friend was getting at when he asked me if I was ever too hard on myself. Maybe he's got a point. I could try the simple slogan he suggested: *Stop!* It sounds like it could help me deal better with my negative self-talk.

When I hear any negative self-talk today,
I will write it down in my notebook
along with a realistic counterthought.

I can share my mistakes and be OK.

It was a while before I could do a Fifth Step—I was afraid I'd be condemned as a bad person. I didn't trust anyone enough.

But I'm glad to say that I was wrong. When I finally did my Fifth Step, I was not rejected or judged, as I thought I would be. Instead, my Fifth Step listener understood me—but more important, she accepted me. I felt relief. I felt humble. I felt grateful.

When I go to sleep tonight, I will say a prayer
to acknowledge my courage and my faith.

I can ask myself: How am I doing?

Before I got into recovery, I didn't want to know what I was feeling or thinking. I couldn't stand to look at my behavior. I was in denial about my co-occurring disorders.

Now I am abstinent and stable—no longer in denial. And I am learning to take care of myself on a daily basis. I realize that I can no longer afford to avoid my thoughts or actions—I might relapse to my addiction or have a setback with my mental disorder. A regular Tenth Step inventory helps me. It teaches me what to *keep* doing to help myself. It also teaches me what to *stop* doing to avoid hurting myself.

> *Today I will set aside five minutes to answer*
> *for myself the question, How am I doing?*

I am slowly recovering my self-respect.

When I was using alcohol and drugs and feeling depressed enough to miss work, I lost interest in most everything. I lost energy and confidence. I often felt guilty, ashamed, and angry.

But since I've stopped drinking and using, I'm feeling better. I have managed to see a psychiatrist and get both medical and psychological treatment for my mental health disorder. I've started going to a support group and a Twelve Step group. In general, I'm seeing how others recover from co-occurring disorders and seeing that I, too, can change my life, little by little, one day at a time.

I will make one change in my day's activities that will help me feel better about myself.

I can start a list of people I have harmed.

I find it hard to acknowledge that I've hurt other people through my co-occurring disorders. It seems I can remember only my own pain, whether due to my addiction or my mental disorder.

But in working the first seven Steps, I see more clearly that, indeed, I have hurt loved ones and others. *It's just hard to admit it.* I'm afraid that if I start thinking about my past behavior, I'll get depressed again or I'll feel guilty enough to drink. I know that I need to be strong and stable when I begin writing the list. And I will trust my Higher Power to help.

> *Today I will start my Eighth Step*
> *by putting just one name on the list.*

I can find acceptance.

I have co-occurring disorders—a substance use disorder and a mental health disorder. Today I am clean and sober, attending outpatient treatment, and taking psychiatric medication. But even though I am taking care of myself, at times I feel ashamed. I feel like hiding. I feel like I'm less than other people—separate and unloved.

Except when I go to my recovery meeting. There, I can be seen and be safe. There, I don't feel judged—we all have similar problems. There, I feel a part of a caring community. They simply accept me with my two no-fault disorders.

I will make a commitment to regularly attend
a Twelve Step meeting such as Dual Recovery
Anonymous so I can be with people who
accept me—the people I need.

I can tell my doctor about my addiction.

When I first saw my psychiatrist about my symptoms, he asked me if I used alcohol or other drugs. For a few moments, I felt ashamed and embarrassed, but I managed to reply that, in fact, I was recovering from alcoholism.

I knew it was important to make this information clear. Because of my addiction, I must abstain from addictive substances. But with a mental health disorder, I might have to take a psychiatric medication, maybe just for a while, perhaps longer term. Happily, I learned that, as long as the medication is not addictive, I am not putting my abstinence at risk. To get stable with my mental disorder, I will not have to risk relapse to my addiction.

Today I will pray for honesty and humility
in all aspects of my recovery.

I want to right my wrongs.

I've done some things in my life that I know hurt other people. Many are minor; a few are major. From time to time, I've been troubled by these regrettable acts. Until recently, I didn't know what I could do about them.

But in the Twelve Step program, there's Step Nine to help me out. It tells me to acknowledge the harm I've done. Chances are that if I apologize and make things right, if I do whatever is necessary, I can feel more at peace with myself. While making amends can be hard at times, I realize now that I can no longer afford a burden of guilt. I can't risk relapse to addiction or to my mental disorder. With the help of my Higher Power, I can do Step Nine.

I can practice making amends by apologizing
the next time I offend someone.

I am learning more about myself.

At first I thought Step Four was only about my guilty deeds. I often felt like skipping my meeting when it came around—I felt guilty enough already without being reminded.

But I have learned that Step Four is useful for more than just recognizing errors and faults. I can use it to recognize my assets too. It is really a tool for simply learning more about myself. And in recovery, I need self-knowledge. Perhaps I'll learn that I have more to offer than I thought.

*I will write out my top two assets on cards
and stick them on my bathroom mirror.*

It will help if I don't compare.

I see my friends with houses and cars. They're raising families, advancing their careers. I want what they have. I deserve what they have. They're not better than I am. This is not fair.

When I get to feeling like this, I know that I'm not accepting myself. It's difficult to do with addiction and mental disorder, but I find I need to do it again and again. No, my friends are not better than I am. No, it is not fair. But *I am who I am:* a good person in recovery from two no-fault disorders. And I am doing the best I can.

Today I will acknowledge my grief
and focus on today's recovery.

I can let go.

I didn't want to work on myself. (I didn't want to admit I had a problem.) I didn't want to accept help. I didn't want to get "better"—because I didn't know what "better" would be like. I was scared and could not trust.

One day I finally told my counselor how scared I was. She looked at me and said, "Yes, I think I understand. And I want to help you." Somehow, I believed her. Somehow, I trusted her. Once I'd told her how I felt, I was able to admit my problems, accept her help—and begin recovery. For that moment, *I let go.* And once I let go, I found a grip.

Today I will give someone a chance
to earn a measure of my trust.

I am willing to change.

Before recovery, the way I was living caused me many problems. Step Six asks me if I'm ready to start changing my life. Can I let go of old ways? Can I learn new coping skills? What am I really willing to do to allow change to happen?

Having done Step Five and dealt with some of the past, there is less to hide, less to be ashamed of, little to hold me back. I feel more open to learning new ways to handle my problems and meet my needs. I feel more open to letting myself be changed. I believe I am now ready to start this process of gradual transformation.

I will say the Serenity Prayer and
I will complete my regular activities
on today's recovery plan.

I stay strong by "carrying the message."

One way I maintain my recovery is to carry the message of recovery to others who still suffer. When I share my experience, strength, and hope with someone who wants help, I recall my own struggles. I remember what has worked for me before and recognize what is working for me today. I stay close to the truth about co-occurring disorders and so stay grateful and humble and strong.

In my recovery I am finding out that the more I give, the more I get; the more I help others, the more I help myself.

I will introduce myself at meetings to
newcomers and make sure my name
is on contact lists.

I am grateful for my helper.

When I first got into treatment, I told my counselor how much I didn't want to go. I insisted I wasn't addicted and that I needed only two things: tranquilizers for my nerves, and freedom.

I'm glad I got this denial and anger out of my system. And I'm grateful for all my counselor's help. First she just listened quietly and patiently. Then, slowly, she let me see that I was scared and in pain. Gently and with understanding, she helped me look at my drug use and my anxiety. She helped me feel better, and then she helped me get on the path of recovery.

> *Today I will thank my helpers and*
> *practice patience with my moods.*

I want to stop feeling sad.

Sometimes I am overwhelmed with sadness. Suddenly I feel alone and helpless. I don't know where it comes from, but I know how much it hurts and frightens me.

I am grateful to my therapist. With his help I am exploring my sore spots, what he calls my buttons, and how they get pushed. It seems that the more I know myself and my moods, the better I can take care of myself. I want to stop feeling so sad, to stabilize my mental health, and avoid a relapse to my addiction.

I will review my day's events and
look for triggers of a sad mood.

*I am learning to deal with a slip
with my mental disorder.*

Yesterday I got extremely upset when I had a serious disagreement with my roommate. I felt angry and sad. When I woke up this morning, I convinced myself I couldn't get out of bed, so I just stayed there until evening.

Tonight I feel a little better, even though we haven't resolved our problem. While I didn't solve it by sleeping, I don't want to be hard on myself for staying in bed so long. It was a slip, and I want to forgive myself for it. Today I see yesterday's events more clearly, and I can see better what I need to do differently tomorrow.

*When I make a mistake today, I will try to
forgive myself and concentrate instead
on the question What can I learn from it?*

I can learn and grow stronger by sitting still.

Now that I've been in recovery for a while, I feel much better. I have added new friends and a support group meeting to my life—very important commitments. But sometimes I feel like I'm too busy—I feel like I'm pushing the river instead of letting it flow.

When I told a friend in my support group about my pace, he offered me a tool called meditation. I listened carefully and learned that instead of trying to grow or change through doing or thinking all the time, one method of meditation is to do *nothing*, to simply sit still and focus on breathing. By sitting quietly and just breathing, it is possible to learn about myself, to slowly, subtly, enhance recovery.

I'll devote five minutes today to
sitting still and just breathing.

I can make a commitment to recovery.

I am coming to believe that there is nothing more important in my life than my recovery—in other words, abstaining from addictive substances and maintaining mental stability. This is because I see myself now as a valuable person who has two disorders and who deserves to be treated well.

One good way to value myself is to devote time each day to my recovery activities. The ones that help me the most are meetings, physical exercise, and spending time with supportive friends. If I do these, I believe that my Higher Power will take care of the rest.

I will make a commitment to recovery
by making a commitment to my
daily recovery plan.

I want a better life for myself.

When I was using drugs and experiencing symptoms of my mental disorder, I cared most about simply staying high, about feeling no pain—whether emotional, physical, or spiritual. My greatest need was a negative one, and I met it with street drugs.

Now that I've achieved a period of abstinence and stability, I can see that there's more to life than just drugs, staying high, and avoiding pain. Some basic, positive needs that I've neglected include healthy food, safe shelter, and clean clothing. In recovery, I am learning that these needs are important and that I can find a way to meet them.

*I will list the five most important things
I need to get along in life.*

I am learning to forgive myself.

I have made many mistakes. I've done things I'm not proud of. I've hurt some people deeply, including myself. This is clear to me today.

But I need to keep in mind that past actions and character defects do not make me a bad person. For my substance use and mental health disorders, I am working a program of co-occurring recovery. Despite my guilt and shame, I am learning to forgive myself. As I see others—friends, therapist, group members—accept me for who I am, I can better accept myself.

> *I will ask my best friend and*
> *my sponsor to help me identify*
> *three of my good qualities.*

APRIL

I need to learn what pushes my buttons.

Not so long ago, I felt trapped in a self-destructive cycle. One day I thought I was fine. The next day I'd end up in detox with mental health symptoms. What was worse is that I couldn't recall what got me to take that first drink. It was frustrating. I felt guilty and ashamed.

At group I'm learning about slips, relapse, and getting my buttons pushed. I know now I need to find out what things upset me and how I "build up to drink." I'm finally learning how to stop this cycle when it starts and then get back on track.

I will ask my counselor or sponsor to help me
figure out the most common things
that lead to a slip for me.

I let in faith when I let go.

It has taken quite a while, but I can now admit that there is a power greater than myself—my co-occurring disorders of addiction and mental disorder. I tried to overcome this disability as best I could with the tools I had, but I could not. Now, instead of fighting my disorders as I did for so long, I am working on accepting them.

And in the process of accepting my disorders, I have discovered an even greater power—my Higher Power. By taking Step One and admitting that I cannot recover on my own, I leave the door open to receive help. I have faith that my Higher Power will give me the help, the tools, I need.

> *Today I will pray the Serenity Prayer and*
> *practice accepting one person or thing*
> *I would otherwise want to change.*

I am looking forward to the future.

The most important thing in my life today is staying abstinent and stable. But being in recovery from co-occurring disorders does not define me for all time. My disorders are only a part of me.

Before I got sick, I was dating and working to advance my career. Now I feel strong enough to get back on track. The track may take a different route—my goals in life have changed some with my disorders—but I still feel I have a lot to contribute to the world—perhaps more now than before.

I will ask my sponsor or therapist to help me
as I make a plan for my future.

I have co-occurring disorders.

I don't want to admit it, but my therapist is right: I have co-occurring disorders. I've used street drugs and alcohol (although I'm clean and sober now), and for the past several months, I have felt depressed, guilty, and exhausted much of the time. I've been sleeping more than usual. I am losing weight. In fact, I'm losing interest in my world.

My co-occurring disorders are very hard to accept. It still scares me to admit that I have two chronic disorders. And yet, in a way, I feel better admitting to these problems. Maybe it's because I'm no longer lying to myself, telling myself these problems aren't problems. Maybe it's because I can now stop fighting and get some relief. And maybe it's because I can now work on recovery instead of covering up.

I will tell my therapist that I am
ready to accept my addiction and
mental health problems.

I am listening to my Higher Power.

I used to fear being alone in a room. It was especially frightening if it was just me and my thoughts—no drugs or alcohol, no books or screens.

But in recovery, I have been learning a way to be by myself: it's called meditation. I go to my quiet place, get comfortable, and then I *stop*. Thoughts pass through my mind but I don't hold on to any of them; I let them come and I let them go. And as my thoughts get quieter, I hear my Higher Power like never before. When meditating, I feel calmer and more accepting.

I will set aside five minutes today
to sit quietly in a quiet place.

I feel a new emotion: joy.

When I was using and having symptoms, it was even hard for me to talk with anyone. I felt too fragile. I feared I would not be understood or accepted. In my struggle, I further isolated myself.

But all that has changed. These days I feel a new freedom. I am sober and stable. My medication is helping (and I can deal with the minor side effects). I feel cared for by my sponsor and therapist. I trust them. In fact, I look forward to my next meetings, where I can talk about my new sense of joy. To me, it seems like a new and wonderful word: *joy.*

> *I will say a prayer of thanks to my*
> *Higher Power and share my joy.*

I'm learning it's OK to cry.

I'm not sure what's going on with me. I know I've been a bit blue for a while now, but I have always felt better sooner or later. These days, when my mood picks up, it is short lived. Soon, I'm weeping again. I'm afraid, and I feel like I'm losing control.

I called my therapist about this again and got some reassurance that what I am feeling is normal and it does not constitute depression. I need to keep reminding myself of her message: *It's OK to cry. It's part of healing.* While it can be frightening to feel so deeply and to feel such deep pain, the feeling alone won't hurt me.

I will make a flash card that reads,
"It's OK to cry and feel the pain."

I must stay free of all addictive substances.

I remember when I finally could admit that I had co-occurring disorders—but was still afraid to stop using alcohol and street drugs. Quitting would mean I would have to go through withdrawal. It would also mean I couldn't manage my emotions the way I used to. Even though it was my choice, I felt defensive and angry.

Fortunately, I remembered to call my psychiatrist and get some support. First, he reassured me that if I needed it, he would help me weather withdrawal. Then he said he would help me find a Twelve Step meeting where I felt comfortable. He emphasized why abstinence is so important to recovery from co-occurring disorders: If I didn't stop using, I could relapse to my addiction and perhaps to my mental health disorder as well. If I used drugs while taking my prescribed medication, I could cause serious medical problems. His knowledge and care helped me to remain stable by getting sober and *staying* sober.

I will find a Twelve Step meeting to attend today.

I am grateful for my life.

I was married. We had a child. I was successful at my job. I felt fulfilled. But then I developed serious mental health problems and addiction. It wasn't long after I started to recover from my co-occurring disorders that my wife and I got divorced.

I don't know how I've managed these life changes, but I now have my feet on solid ground. And I only know that regularly I have called on my Higher Power, and regularly I have called on the combined experience, strength, and hope of my helpers in my Twelve Step and other support groups. For giving me hope, for saving my life, I am deeply grateful to them all.

Today I will work Step Twelve and carry
the message of recovery with gratitude
and humility.

I can call my doctor when I need to.

After being assessed for medication, I was given the prescription, told how to take it, and told to check in with my doctor if I had any problems. I took the medicine as prescribed, but after a day or two, my hands got shaky, my mouth got dry, and I felt nauseated.

I wasn't sure if I should call. My psychiatrist is very busy and has many patients, and I didn't want to cause any fuss. But eventually I did call, and sure enough, she thanked me for the report. She prescribed a change in the dosage and asked me to call back if things didn't improve. Fortunately, the adjustment helped, and in this process, I learned another way to take care of myself.

If I have questions about my medication,
or if things don't seem right, I will call
my doctor or therapist.

I can handle my changes.

I'm not using alcohol or drugs these days, and I'm getting help for my depression. Overall I feel much better (although the side effects of the medication are a nuisance). But so much is changing. Sometimes I don't feel like myself or I wonder about who I am. (Is this due to the medication?) I feel, in a word, unsettled.

It helped when I brought this up with my doctor. She understood and supported me, saying that recovery is very unsettling and uncomfortable for *everyone*. It will get better over time, she added, especially once the medication is optimized. Knowing how normal I am makes this stage much easier for me to accept.

I will talk with two members of my support group today about how they handled all the changes of recovery from co-occurring disorders.

I am OK when I make a mistake.

Growing up I learned that it was important to look strong at all times. I even learned not to apologize. Yet sometimes I did things that I felt bad about. But to acknowledge them was to look weak and perhaps to risk attack.

In recovery I am learning new ideas, new ways. I am learning that it's OK to acknowledge mistakes. I'm finding out that if I say "I'm sorry," my guilt diminishes. When I make a mistake in recovery, I no longer feel angry at myself or assume that I'm bad or weak. Instead, I see myself as someone who can make a mistake, learn from it, and then be willing to change. It's good to know I'm human.

I will pray for strength to accept myself
and admit my mistakes.

I am trying to accept my medication.

I'm not yet comfortable with my medications for my mental health disorder. But I don't know which is worse—feeling sad and anxious without the medication or feeling out of touch, thirsty, and constipated due to the side effects. It seems there are problems either way. I guess I thought the medication would just take care of everything.

So my doctor and I talked again about the side effects. We also talked about how this medicine helps—much like a pair of eyeglasses—but does not cure, and how I still have to do *my* part to recover. I trust my doctor. Working together with him, I believe that slowly, things will improve all around.

*I will ask my Higher Power for willingness
and for patience.*

· APRIL 14 ·

I am grateful for a good night's rest.

I had not been sleeping well for a while. Every night I would toss and turn. Then I'd wake up and try to fall back to sleep by watching TV or reading. It was hard to relax when I was so frustrated.

But I'm sleeping better now. I've made progress in therapy and got some good tips from my doctor—for example, get some exercise, take your meds at bedtime, avoid caffeine or cigarettes before bed. Sometimes it still takes a while to fall asleep, and sometimes I still have troubling dreams. But usually I make it through the night without waking up. And for this I am deeply grateful. It sounds simple, but getting a good night's sleep means a lot to me in my recovery.

*I will thank my Higher Power for my rest
and carefully follow my doctor's tips
to improve my sleep.*

I need to channel my anger.

I have a short fuse again these days. Suddenly I feel like I want to explode, like I want to smash things. I wish I knew what sets me off—work? my disorders? I don't feel like myself. It scares me and I wish I could cool off.

When I told my therapist I was concerned about my strong feelings, she began by assuring me that it's OK to be angry, for whatever reason. She explained that anger itself is not an issue, it's what I do with it. Then we explored ways to release my anger in order to stay balanced, safe, and strong. Dealing with resentment and anger are important issues in my recovery.

I will ask my higher helper for courage
to accept my anger and deal with it
in a healthy way.

I am accepting my co-occurring disorders.

I know I have an addiction, and I know that addiction is a disorder, a disease. But it's hard for me to believe that I have an "mental" disorder. I always pictured such people in a hospital or institution. I thought of them as "crazy."

These days I am finding out how mistaken I've been. Such people are *not* crazy; they're *not* always in a hospital or institutionalized. More likely, they're with me at work, with me at the store, with me in church. They are like me and I am like them. *In fact, I am one of them.*

I will write out an affirmation that reads,
"I am more like other people than I am different."

I can't help it, I'm changing.

When I relapsed, I was despondent. I had done all I could do to stay abstinent and stable. I believed that since nothing had worked for me, nothing *would* work for me. I was tired of trying and tired of holding on. I gave up.

However, in giving up I learned an important concept: *I cannot control change.* As hard as I might try, I cannot make change happen. As hard as I might try, I cannot stop change from happening. This makes me more willing to be patient, more willing to let time help the healing. Life is change. And though I may struggle and feel like a failure, I am, in fact, changing. Being patient, holding on, is an important part of change.

Today I will do what I can for my recovery—
and then let go of trying to control change.

I am searching for strength and meaning.

It is hard to face my uncertain future. With my co-occurring disorders, especially the mood disorder, I now see that much in my life must change in order to get better. Sometimes I feel I have little to hold on to.

But no matter what else changes, I will always have the Twelve Step program. It does not predict the course of my recovery, but it offers me bedrock to stand on, a path to follow, and the understanding and strength of fellow travelers. It offers me meaning.

I will attend at least two Twelve Step
meetings each week as part of my
co-occurring recovery plan.

I don't want to hurt myself anymore.

I used to have painful episodes in which I would end up physically hurting myself. External events and internal thoughts would generate extreme distress, even rage. The only way I could think of to find relief (surprising as it seems to me now) was to hurt myself. Somehow at the time, it helped.

These days, I am learning other ways to release my pain, to channel my rage. For one, I'm talking about my feelings with helpful people. For another, I'm hitting tennis balls (instead of myself). Now when I feel that intensity rise, I am less afraid and less at risk. I have choices.

If I ever feel self-destructive, I will practice one of the techniques I've learned to relieve the pain and soothe myself.

I want to have faith.

At my Twelve Step meeting, I hear the word *faith*. I hear that it's important to my recovery. It's a small word, but I don't think I understand it. And I don't think I have much of it.

And yet, as a child, I remember my uncle would hold my hands and wrists tight and swing me around and around and around. It scared me, but I loved it. I giggled. I got dizzy. I squealed in delight. Then, smiling, he would slow the spinning and slowly let me down. *I trusted him and he never dropped me.* Is that what faith is about?

*I will ask two of my friends at group
to talk with me about who they trust
and what they believe in.*

I want to relax more with people.

In treatment it was painful to sit in a circle at group at first. Everybody could see me. I couldn't hide or get away. Sometimes I even had to talk. I was afraid people wouldn't like me or understand me (and then would look at me funny).

But after being with the group for several sessions, I was able to glance up at my fellow members when I was talking. Guess what? Nobody was looking at me funny at all. I think most were looking within themselves. After that, group got easier for me. Being able to talk in group has helped a lot.

> Today I'll practice looking at the person
> I am talking to (knowing I can look away
> at any time and feel safer).

I am grateful for the telephone.

I don't know where my recovery would be without my phone. In just a few seconds I can get support from a sponsor, friend, or counselor. I don't have to feel isolated when I have or am near a phone. It is comforting and reassuring, especially when I'm having symptoms.

Although it's not the same as meeting with someone in person (or going to a recovery meeting), it is a powerful substitute that allows me to have a heart-to-heart talk with a caring person. It works well for me (especially when I'm too sick to get out). I am grateful that I am almost always able to connect with others.

I will meditate today on my network
of friends and on how (and when)
I connect with them.

*I have co-occurring disorders,
two chronic disorders like diabetes.*

I wonder if having co-occurring disorders is like having other chronic diseases, say, like diabetes. Having co-occurring disorders makes me feel different, excluded, self-conscious. Sometimes it's even hard to face people. Some seem afraid of me. They don't understand my addiction and mental health problems.

But these are no-fault disorders, and I am just like people with diabetes. I need professional help, just like people with diabetes. I deserve to be treated with respect and understanding, just like people with diabetes. I am in recovery—just like people diagnosed with diabetes.

*When I feel stigmatized, I will call a friend
for reassurance and support.*

I can help myself by taking medication.

I did not want to take psychiatric medication for three reasons: I didn't want to admit the seriousness of my problem; I didn't want to feel ashamed; I didn't trust it.

For a long time I fought the idea—and then I hit a bottom. I realized that although counseling was helping, it wasn't working fast enough. I didn't have to keep suffering such intense and disabling feelings. I feared that if I didn't get stable, I might need to be hospitalized. By taking prescribed medication, I saw that I would be taking good care of myself.

I will carefully follow my medication
instructions and thank my
Higher Power for this kind of help.

I am finding the help I need.

I managed to stop using and get my mental health symptoms under control in treatment. But once out, I wasn't sure I could *stay* straight and stable. I was afraid I would get sick again under stress or with strong cravings. I was afraid I couldn't manage on my own.

But finally, when the fear got strong enough, I went to a recovery meeting to look for help. And over the course of several weeks, I could tell that I had found it: the consistency, structure, and spirituality of the meeting itself combined with the respectful, caring, and consistent support of a sponsor (or guide, mentor, helper). I now had one way to help me manage my disability on my own.

I will write down two reasons why
I need help to recover and the name
of someone who can help me.

My emotions are connected to my body.

It started when I was a child: whenever I felt sick to my stomach, I got sad and scared. I had an emotional reaction to what was going on in my body. In short, I felt awful.

In recovery, I notice this pattern in reverse: I have a physical reaction to my emotions. When I get upset or feel depressed, I may quickly feel tired and achy. Sometimes I even get a stomachache (although I no longer use drugs or alcohol). But I don't feel awful. The difference is that over time I have learned that my mood affects the way my body feels, just as my body affects my mood. Understanding this important relationship helps me stay focused on the problem.

Three times today I will note my mood
and how my body feels.

I can expect to feel some ups and downs.

I thought that once I got sober and once my medication took effect, I'd be OK. I do feel better, but I still have some hard days that I didn't expect. They scare me—they remind me of how much I struggled with my addiction and mental health problems before I sought help. Sometimes I feel like I'm right back at the bottom.

And yet, after the wave of fear diminishes, I remember that I am now on the right path and I am not alone. I need to keep in mind that since my co-occurring disorders developed over time, it may take some time to cope with them. Having two chronic disorders is not a simple problem.

I will ask my Higher Power for strength
and patience to help me stay balanced.

My program provides helpful tools for recovery.

At first I thought that all I had to do was join a Twelve Step fellowship and my problems would be solved. I even thought (hoped?) that twelve meetings (one for each Step) would do the trick. But what I found out was that the program does not *cure* a chronic disorder. However, using some simple yet powerful tools can help me *recover* one day at a time.

There are several of them, and they're used in all the fellowships. The tools include meetings, service, accountability (inventories, amends), the literature, prayer, meditation, the phone, the Steps, the Traditions, and anonymity. In my program these days, I use at least one of them every day to help me stay free of alcohol and drugs and stay stable in my mental health.

Today I will practice using one recovery
tool on a current problem.

I need a quiet place.

These days I'm sober, stable—and fragile. My therapy is helping me get better, but it's also stressful and upsetting. Emotionally, I feel bruised and raw. I also feel sad at times because it seems there are few people in my life who understand me and the process of recovery from co-occurring disorders.

Because I am working hard on my recovery each day, I need a place of serenity and safety. I am learning that a quiet retreat can help me regain strength, get centered, and do the private healing I need. It's one of the important new ways I am learning to take care of myself in recovery.

I will find or make a place where I can go
at any time for safety, release, and relief.

I deserve respect.

People with heart disease or diabetes need not be secretive about their disorder to avoid stigma. They are not looked down on for having a serious disorder. In short, they are respectfully supported throughout their disorder.

In the same spirit, I need to be treated with respect as I heal from my addiction and mental disorder. I need to be understood as a good person who has two no-fault disorders and who is doing the best he can. (And yet, there may be times when I need to protect myself from people who are judgmental and insensitive.) However, I am discovering that the more I respect myself, the more others will respect me.

> *Today I will acknowledge my ongoing*
> *recovery and try my best to accept*
> *those who don't accept me.*

MAY

I can manage my feelings of guilt.

There were times when I felt so guilty that I (*a*) used drugs just to forget the pain, (*b*) couldn't be around people, or (*c*) hurt myself and even thought of suicide. I considered myself a bad person and knew of no way to change.

I still think of using sometimes when I feel guilty. But I don't—because as I am in recovery from co-occurring disorders I am taking three facts to heart: I have two *no-fault* disorders, I tend to be hard on myself, and I am a *good* person who deserves love and health. In recovery, I am learning that my feelings of guilt diminish when I work my program (for instance, by doing a Fourth Step and a Fifth Step) and stay honest doing a daily Tenth Step inventory. The relief, the peace, are worth it.

Today I will do an anonymous
favor for someone.

I know now I have a problem with alcohol.

I could accept the fact that I had a mental disorder, and I was able to manage it (I took my medication as prescribed). But I didn't agree that I had an addiction. When I drank, I usually had just one, because I thought I knew my limit. Alcohol seemed to affect me little. I wanted people to just leave me alone about this.

But once I thought about it, I realized it had become harder to stop at "just one." Then it became harder to stop at two—especially the nights I got drunk. I was feeling more tense and irritable, and I found myself thinking about drinking more and more. Fortunately, my doctor suggested that alcohol was probably affecting me more than I realized. I'm glad I listened to her and got help before my addiction progressed further.

I will call my doctor, therapist, or sponsor
when I still have doubts about drinking.

I have much to offer.

Deep down I used to think of myself as a sick and defective person in a life that could not be changed. I thought I was someone who could not take responsibility, who could not hold a job, who just kept making the same mistakes, as if I didn't know better.

Getting a hold on my co-occurring disorders has been a struggle, but after some months now in recovery, I feel stronger, resilient, even courageous. With my abstinence and stability, I can see that I do not have to be limited by my problems: I am not just a person with co-occurring disorders. I have abilities and I am learning how to put them to use as I heal. These days I sense that I can do whatever is needed, not just to take care of myself, but to flourish.

*Today I will make a list of my
strengths, my assets.*

I didn't cause them and I can't cure them.

I used to feel frustrated and disappointed with myself after having symptoms of my mental health disorder. Sometimes I got drunk to take the edge off the symptoms. But when I woke up with a hangover, I felt guilty and ashamed. I felt as though I had given up some control.

I still experience some of these feelings at times, but since I stopped drinking, my life feels more manageable. Learning about my co-occurring disorders has also helped. While these two biological disorders are not my fault, I am responsible for dealing with them: (a) I need to stay clean and sober, (b) I need to take my medication as prescribed by my psychiatrist, and (c) I need to attend a support group for my mental health issues and a Twelve Step group for my addiction. If I do these things, I will be taking good care of myself in recovery.

Today I will ask my Higher Power for self-acceptance and my psychiatrist for information about my disorders.

· MAY 5 ·

I am forgiving myself.

Without the understanding and strength I gained doing the first three Steps, I couldn't have begun to work Step Four. Here, I start to look at the people I have hurt—myself among them—and the damage I have done. It is a difficult process that I wish I could put off. But I cannot.

Sometimes I feel bad about myself during this "fearless and searching" review. But it will help if I work on Step Four a little at a time and remind myself that what I am doing in the program is the best thing I have ever done for myself (or others). *I am changing, growing, recovering.* Knowing that I'm doing what I need to do and feeling better gives me strength for my Fourth Step inventory.

I will work a little on Step Four today and
write out an affirmation that reads,
"I am learning to accept and forgive myself."

I know now how treatment has helped.

I didn't want to be in treatment. I was afraid to have to work on both my addiction and mental disorders. I didn't think it would help. I didn't know anybody, and everybody looked strange to me. For the first few days, I tried to get out and go home (such as it was).

But once I settled down a little, I could see that being away from my daily routine was helpful. I relaxed a little and got to where I could concentrate better. I got to a place where I felt much less tempted to use and was taking my medication regularly. The best part, however, was that I started meeting people with problems like mine, people who tried to understand me. All this has helped.

*Today I will remember two things I learned
in treatment that have helped.*

I can make it through the pain.

I can't relax. I feel sad and I'm angry at myself. It's hard to concentrate, especially at work. Sometimes my mind goes blank. I keep forgetting things.

My friends tell me that such emotions are not uncommon in recovery for co-occurring disorders. (I thought I was the only one who had ever felt this way.) Quitting an addiction and starting therapy for mental health problems are powerful changes. It's reassuring when they say that I am not "crazy" (I just feel like it) and that in a couple of weeks the medication I started will help me to settle down (although I would prefer the pain to go away *now*). I am grateful to my friends, especially because they keep telling me, "You can get through the pain." Yes, I *can* get through the pain.

I will take two walks today and jot down
two activities I can do with my hands.

I am letting go of my low mood.

I feel somewhat better this week. It is hard to describe (and it doesn't quite make sense), but it feels like I am actually getting tired of being depressed. I feel worn out, as if purged of pain.

Even though I still have some symptoms to deal with, I believe that, for the first time, I can see light at the end of the tunnel. I can see that I am less obsessed with my problems. Maybe I can let go of some of this heaviness and darkness. It would be a relief.

I will do one fun activity today and wear
bright clothes to enhance my spirits.

I need to use my support network.

I sit at home, watch TV, and eat. I can't concentrate enough to read. And I can't stop thinking. At night sometimes, I'm too agitated to sleep. When I wake up, I feel exhausted. I have little energy.

Those are the longest days and longest nights. And yet I know I don't have to be alone or cope all by myself. If I work up the courage, I can go to a recovery meeting, talk with a friend on the phone, walk with a friend, or get in touch with my sponsor or counselor. I know that when I spend time with others in recovery, it's easier to spend time with myself.

Today I will contact two support people,
one during the day and one in the evening.

I am coming alive in recovery.

Lately when I awaken, I feel stronger, hopeful, willing. I have a sense of purpose these days—to recover from my co-occurring disorders, to reclaim my life—and I know what I need to do.

I have come out from under the rock. I feel free and light. With my recovery plan to guide me, my days are full and I sleep well at night. I feel grateful to my Higher Power for this new strength and spirit.

I will quietly share my process and my joy
with my sponsor and group.

I want to talk about my problems.

I suspected I had some problems with my emotions and my drinking. But I was too confused and ashamed to talk with anyone about them. And yet I wanted to. It was frightening to feel out of control, to mistrust everyone. I didn't want to feel alone. I wanted someone to know what was happening with me.

With the help of some "luck," what I now call my Higher Power, a trusting friend told me about his recovery in AA. I am deeply grateful for his introduction to this fellowship. I now see that there are others like me, others who can help me simply by their example, by listening to me, and by accepting me. This is what I need to continue coming out of isolation.

I will check in with my sponsor today
and allow time for a fellow member
who might need my support.

I need a guide.

In the past my only guide was myself (and my addiction). I did the best I could with what I had, but it wasn't nearly what I needed to manage co-occurring disorders. And I was not willing to accept ideas for change that weren't my own.

Now, after a lengthy journey, I have found a new guide, a source of wisdom and strength much greater than myself. I freely choose this Higher Power, which includes the Twelve Step program. As difficult as it is to do at times, I am letting go of my old unsuccessful ways of coping and I'm trusting more in my Higher Power. I have found a better way, and I will make it a serious commitment.

I will write down one way in which I have already "let go" in my recovery.

I am grateful for the Twelve Steps.

Long ago I gave up my initial guide to living, the religion of my childhood. But the spiritual crisis of my co-occurring disorders left me desperate, lost. I did not know what to do.

After a period of struggle, I found the Twelve Steps—and I am profoundly grateful. The Steps are *spiritual*, not religious. They are *gentle, forgiving*. They make it possible for me to recover. They help me accept myself and others. They help me live the kind of life I want. The Twelve Steps are at work in my life.

Today I will spend ten minutes reading about
and thinking about this week's Step.

I can see that my life has meaning.

Lately I've been feeling sorry for myself and what I've had to go through. Addiction and a mental health disorder are terrible disorders to suffer. I feel sad about my losses—why *me?*—and then I get angry.

But at least I am not harboring my emotions these days. Instead, I talk about them with my sponsor. When I told her about the pity, she suggested I reread the Promises in the Big Book (pp. 83–84). By accepting her advice, I was gently reminded that despite sorrow and suffering, *my life has meaning.* I realize that I am becoming a more spiritual person. And through my recovery, I can help others recover too.

I will pray for steadiness in my recovery
and carry the message of hope
to others who still suffer.

I need to keep trying.

Right now, I don't much care. I've been straight and had slips. I've been stable and had setbacks. I'm tired of getting up and falling down. Lately it feels like I'm losing control again. I'm afraid I have a long way to go in my recovery.

And yet now that I know what recovery feels like, I know I want it, and I know how to get there. I know, too, that if I think about past events too much, I may get discouraged and do nothing. It's hard to accept that recovery is a process—but I want to get back on track. I will not quit trying.

*Today I will attend a recovery meeting
and contact my sponsor (or therapist)
for extra support.*

I am right where I am supposed to be.

Here I am, a few months sober, wondering if the cravings will get me, wondering if my lingering depression will drag me down, wondering what's happening to my life.

As difficult as it is for me to accept at times, I have co-occurring disorders—and there are no simple answers. My tasks are to learn about my disorders, work a program of co-occurring recovery (including taking medication, as prescribed), and avoid relapse. The more I accept these tasks, the more I believe that my life will follow its true path.

I will carry out each activity
on today's recovery plan.

I can't quit my meds just yet.

I don't like taking my psychiatric medication. I don't have insurance, and I don't have the money to keep buying it. Besides I've been taking it long enough—I feel better now. Sometimes I forget to take it anyway, and it doesn't seem to make any difference.

Yet as much as I want to just quit, I have to keep in mind what my doctor told me when I got to this point before. (If I do, I'll probably save myself additional misery.) (a) Since my medication has long-lasting effects, I might not notice a missed pill here and there, but I would notice several pills missed in a row; (b) when I go off medication, it's medically critical to taper it; and (c) most important, even though I'm feeling better, I need to stay on my medication a while longer to prevent a setback or a relapse to addiction.

If I want to make any changes in my medication,
I will be sure to contact my doctor.

What am I feeling right now?

For me, the first stage in recovery from my co-occurring disorders was getting abstinent. The second stage is getting stable with my mental disorder (while remaining abstinent).

To progress in psychological recovery—now that I am sober—I want to know my true feelings. I want names for them and I want to understand them. I don't want them to result in mood swings (or binges). I want to accept them. I want to deal with them in a healthy way. In sum, I want emotional stability.

> *I will stop twice today to jot down how*
> *I am feeling or what I am feeling.*

I can deal with this slip.

I feel guilty. I feel ashamed. Right now, I loathe myself for having had a slip. Things were going along fine—my Twelve Step meetings, meds, outpatient treatment—and then I woke up with a hangover. What happened? What did I do? I feel like crawling under a rock.

And yet—*I've come this far.* I know what it's like to be sober and stable. And I know what to do to stay sober and stable. I don't want to let this slip turn into a full-blown relapse. I don't want to slip back into the chaos of the old days, before I got help for my co-occurring disorders. What I need now is prayer and a little more help.

I will talk with my sponsor to help me
forgive myself and to explore
what led up to the slip.

I am beginning to see improvement.

I realize that recovery is a slow, subtle process with periods of growth and then plateaus. But over the past few weeks I am happy to see improvement in the three areas of my life affected by my co-occurring disorders: I feel less irritable and more patient (emotional); I am sleeping better and my stomach trouble has cleared up (physical); I've settled on a home group, and I now have a sponsor (spiritual).

I am grateful to claim another chip at my Twelve Step meeting this month. It helps me see that I can change, that my life is getting better, and that the program truly works.

I will tell my group (or sponsor) about the two most important things I did during the past month to help myself recover.

The Twelve Steps are important to me.

Soon after I left home, I stopped going to church. With mental disorders and addiction in my family—and little spiritual foundation of my own—I soon felt lost and alone in the world. Eventually I became addicted and developed a mental health disorder.

But in recovery for my co-occurring disorders, once again I have a spiritual guide, the Twelve Steps. They are simple, affirming, and practical. They ask only that I seek sobriety and stability. And yet I find that the more I embrace the Steps and a sober, spiritual life, the more I get out of them. Had I not found them, I might have lost my life altogether. I am deeply grateful for these Steps.

At my meeting I will share how the
Twelve Steps have begun to restore my life,
spiritually and emotionally.

I know now who I am.

I realize that I am willing to believe others' opinions of me before my own. I am too willing to doubt myself. And whether intentionally or not, maliciously or not, people can easily be critical of me.

But now that I've done a Fourth and a Fifth Step, I know better what my weaknesses are (as well as my strengths). I know better what to do in order to accept myself and what to work on in order to change. I'm glad I've evaluated myself on my own. And I thank my Higher Power for giving me the strength to do so.

*I will write affirmations on two
of my strong points and tape them
to my bathroom mirror.*

I can resist the urge to use.

I think I won't survive if I don't have my drug. I think that if I can't use, I'll scream or smash something. I think I actually ache; it feels like I'm losing control.

And then suddenly I remember what I've learned from my counselor and sponsor—if I hold off, *the cravings will pass.* They say that if I can distract myself for just four or five minutes, I will be OK. I believe my helpers (although each minute can feel like an hour). I want recovery badly. I can do what it takes to stay clean and sober.

*I will pray for strength and courage. I will
call my sponsor (or friend) as soon as
I feel the urge to use.*

Recovery is my first priority.

When I was in treatment for my co-occurring disorders, I would rather have been at work. I was surprised how much I missed my job and my co-workers. There were the unpaid bills and, of course, the uncertainty of my future.

It's still hard for me to take the time to deal with these disorders. But as I feel better—and I *continue to* feel better—it gets easier for me to see that career and money aren't everything. I trust that I will be healthier and happier in the long run if I deal with these disorders as needed. And I realize that it takes time. But *recovery* is my first priority.

I will pray for strength to let go of my fears
and clarity to focus on my recovery.

I am learning to cry.

Feeling sad and alone was terrible. But I felt even worse when I wanted to cry and was afraid to. I was afraid of feeling so much pain at once that I wouldn't be able to stand it. I was afraid that if I let my emotions out, no one would pay attention and I would be left alone with them.

Eventually, during a session with my therapist, I could no longer hold back the pain and the tears came. At first I felt overwhelmed, then angry, then sad. After a while, I finally felt some relief. By no longer holding in my strong feelings, I can see that they are valid and honorable, and that they will not destroy me.

I will look for a safe place to cry, and when needed, a safe person to cry with.

By accepting my past, I accept my present.

I grew up in a household dominated by a parent with a severe addiction and mental disorder. There was too little security or love or food. I was a child—helpless and stuck.

In recovery from my own co-occurring disorders, I am discovering that while I cannot change the past, I can try to understand it and learn from it. As my past becomes clearer to me, my life—and how I experience it—appear in a new light. For example, I can now reexamine my rigidity, perfectionism, and especially my fear of change. As I accept my past and its lessons, I come to accept my present (and myself) more.

I will ask my counselor to help me
explore my family of origin.

I want to feel closer to my Higher Power.

I am working on the prayer and meditation Step, Step Eleven, and I have two problems: (*a*) The only prayers I know (learned in childhood) are not part of me anymore and (*b*) I am uncomfortable with the idea of meditation because I don't like silence or being alone. Yet I *want* to become more spiritual and feel more connected to my Higher Power.

Fortunately, what I hear from my fellow members is that it's important to find my own ways to connect with my Higher Power—there are many ways—and prayer and meditation are only suggestions. One person suggested that simply making a phone call to give or receive support could be considered a form of prayer. I appreciate such ideas. Perhaps I am already closer to my Higher Power than I thought.

> *Today I will take ten minutes to ask myself*
> *two questions: What is my Higher Power?*
> *And when (and how) do I feel connected*
> *to my Higher Power?*

I am becoming more honest.

Rejection hurts, and I've had enough of it. I want people to like me. I don't want to feel alone. The problem is that if somebody is mad at me, I may apologize even though I've done little or nothing wrong. Or I may say yes to someone just because I'm afraid to say no. Both situations cause me shame and anger when I think about them.

Through therapy and my program, however, I am coming to see how important it is to be honest. Basically, I need to say what I am feeling, to be straightforward. And I am discovering that people accept me, for instance, even when I disagree with them, even when I tell them no. In fact, some people not only accept me, they come to respect me. Honesty works.

I will enlist support when I am
afraid to speak my mind.

I need to make a relapse prevention plan.

I am not used to making plans—unless it's planning to stay high or get high again. Often it's been hard for me to slow down and think things through.

   Coming into recovery I have seen that relapse can happen to *any* of us. I don't like to think about being back where I was. I don't want to feel the pain of relapse. So it seems like a good idea to make a relapse prevention plan—a just-in-case plan, a form of insurance. If I should have a slip (a lapse) at some point, it will help me get back on track faster.

I will ask my therapist and sponsor to help me develop a relapse prevention plan.

I can manage intense feelings.

It seems that my drug use masked a lot of my feelings. And now that I've been clean and sober for a few weeks, I'm flooded with emotions: guilt, shame, fear, anger, self-pity, and more. At times I can't think straight. (At times I can't think.) Everything seems to be coming at me at once.

When I called my sponsor, he agreed that this isn't an easy time and he reassured me that my experience is normal for early recovery. While easier said than done, he thought it might help to practice allowing the feelings to pass through, without fighting them too hard. But most important, he reminded me that I am sane and sober and getting better. At that very point, I *felt* better. I am grateful for my sponsor, and I am learning to trust him.

> *I will practice a regular exercise routine*
> *and check in regularly with my sponsor.*

I need to stay in touch with people.

I'm not behaving the way I really want to these days. It's like when I used to get drunk or high regularly and then act out. I feel like I'm making the same mistakes. I keep making people mad at me. Sometimes I think it would be better if I didn't see anyone or even talk to anyone.

But that's not what I hear in my support group. They say that if I talk about my behavior and my feelings, if I let out some of the hurt, I will feel better. It's when I keep the feelings inside that I start to spiral down. To be open or ask for help right now is hard for me, yet it looks like that's what I need to do for my recovery.

I will be sure to get in touch, and stay
in touch, with my counselor, sponsor,
or a trusted friend.

JUNE

I can take a time out.

It's late. I'm tired and in a bad mood. I'm paying bills, and I'm getting more and more irritated as I open them—especially the statements from my psychiatrist, therapist, and insurance company. I'm ready to fling the pen across the room.

I clench the pen in my fist, clench my teeth, raise my arm—and stop. Suddenly, I *realize* that I am angry—and not so much at the bills but at my co-occurring disorders and at the mistakes I've made. It's not easy taking responsibility for my actions and making a commitment to recovery. I think what I need to do right now is to take a break and sort through these strong emotions.

> *Today I will practice the slogan HALT:*
> *I will avoid getting too hungry,*
> *angry, lonely, or tired.*

I truly feel accepted at a meeting.

While they have been supportive, I am sure my family members are weary of dealing with my emotional problems. My colleagues, though they know little, are suspicious, and I'm not surprised that they object to my moodiness, irritability, and frequent absences. But at my meeting, it's altogether a different story.

I notice it as I walk into the room. I see friendly and familiar faces. I see people I am learning to trust, even though I don't know them well. It feels wonderful. I relax and breathe deeper. I think more clearly, even though some thoughts are painful. I look forward to going back each week, and I sense that the other group members want me to come back too.

> *Just as I have been welcomed and*
> *accepted, I will do service for my group*
> *and welcome newcomers.*

I am becoming willing to ask for help.

I feel so anxious, I'm pacing. I feel panicky. (Drinking used to help, but I am sober now.) I'm afraid that if I sit down, I'll become paralyzed. I'm not sure I can call for help. Would anybody understand? Could anybody really help?

And yet I don't think I can handle all this on my own anymore. I don't think I *should* try to manage this alone anymore. I'm tired of this fear and isolation. I feel desperate—like I did just before I stopped using. Perhaps—perhaps I *can* reach out for help. I did it once before, for my addiction. Maybe I can do it again.

I will now pick up the phone and
dial the number of a trusted friend.

I am OK.

I feel ashamed and small at times: stereotypes are hard to fight. Some people think that everyone with a mental health problem behaves bizarrely, looks odd, or is stuck in a hospital.

But it's not true. I have a mental health problem and I am in recovery. I hold a steady job, I provide for my family, and I look like most of the other fathers on my block (except for the ones with more hair!). I believe that I am more *like* everyone else than I am different. And what's more important is that no matter what anyone else says (or thinks), *I am OK.*

I will list two ways that I am like everyone else or two ways that I am OK.

My appearance is important to me now.

When I was using drugs and having serious symptoms, I didn't much care what happened to me—except that I stayed high as long as I could. And I didn't much care about how I looked to anyone else. It didn't matter.

But with a little abstinence and stability, I care about myself more. I feel a new respect for myself that includes my body and especially my face. In recovery it's important to me that I look OK. When I take care of my appearance, I feel better about myself.

Today I will shower, comb my hair,
and put on clean clothes.

It's OK to talk about my problems.

I used to talk about my problems all the time. I was anxious and depressed and scared. I didn't know what to do to help myself. Eventually, I got on people's nerves (and they told me so). Sometimes I felt rejected and shut out from sources of help.

But slowly I've learned four pertinent truths for my recovery from co-occurring disorders: (*a*) When I talk about my spiritual, physical, or mental pain, I tend to accept it more, and then I can usually do something about it. (*b*) I need to pick the right person and the right time to talk. (*c*) Sometimes I complain too much, when what I really need to do is take more responsibility for myself. (*d*) A sense of humor is a gift.

Today I will pray for willingness
and perspective.

I am not alone anymore.

It's hard for me to be alone. I can feel paralyzed if I even think about it too long, especially when I recall some of my darkest days. Being isolated is part of what got me into treatment in the first place—that and staying drunk all the time.

Being in a day treatment program helped me feel better. It was good to be with other recovering people much of the day, people who generally understood me, who accepted me and supported me. I feel stronger, more independent, and grateful for this help.

*Tonight I will call and chat with a friend
from my treatment program.*

I am doing the best I can.

I want to get well. I want to recover, but I keep sliding back into my old pattern. I start feeling overwhelmed by my problems, get depressed, and then have a slip. I feel bad that I can't get a handle on this. I thought I knew what to do, but what I'm doing is not working.

When I told my support group about this, they reminded me of two things: (a) Slips don't have to be such a bad thing. A slip says that I need to make some changes in my relapse prevention program. (b) Recovery is a process that takes time and forgiveness. When I can think about it that way, I'm not so hard on myself and I can do what I need to do.

I will ask my group and counselor
to help me identify my warning signs
that precede a slip.

I am learning about making mistakes.

I used to feel awful about myself when I made a mistake (and for some time afterward). For example, a mistake in my recovery for co-occurring disorders might be forgetting to go to a meeting or take my meds; it might be getting upset out of proportion to a problem. Simply having symptoms felt like a mistake to me. (At times, I felt like *I* was the mistake.) I felt less than other people for having a mental disorder.

Now I treat myself more gently. Recovery is teaching me to do that. I work on forgiving myself as soon as I can after making a mistake. I'm learning that everyone, even people I look up to, makes mistakes (including my therapist and sponsor). In fact, making a mistake may be the most common way to learn—it tells me I need to do something different.

I will recall my last mistake and
write down two lessons I can learn,
or have learned, from it.

I want to know my moods.

I'm not sure what's going on. I worry that I'm heading for more problems. Even though I'm abstinent, going to meetings, and taking my meds, I have these bleak stretches that last two or three days. They're getting me down.

But a fellow program member gave me a good tip. She said that when she feels bad and doesn't know why, she takes time out to carefully review the day (or the past couple of days). She lists each emotionally significant event and asks herself how she feels about it, particularly about her part in it. We talked further, and I saw how this process could help me learn what I've been thinking, so I can understand what I'm feeling. Then I'll be able to decide what, if anything, to do next.

Today I will sit down for five minutes
to practice listening to my thinking and
try to learn what I'm feeling.

I want to become more assertive.

One important issue I am working on in my recovery from co-occurring disorders is assertiveness. I am tired of the anger and shame I feel when I don't speak up for myself or when I don't say what I want.

I believe I'm *afraid* to speak up—perhaps because I'm afraid that if I do, I'll hurt someone or perhaps *I'll* end up being hurt or rejected (or even emotionally attacked). But through my support groups I'm learning two big things: (*a*) I have more courage and strength than I thought and (*b*) people can take care of themselves.

> *I will practice saying what I think and what*
> *I want with two safe people: for starters,*
> *my therapist and my sponsor.*

I am slowly accepting myself.

With my co-occurring disorders it seems I have lost some of my abilities. I can't concentrate, sleep, or remember as well these days. There are times I can't go to work, eat my regular foods, or even drive a car.

I can't do much of anything except work on my recovery. That's hard—but it's also good. Because in my heart I know that recovery is what I need to concentrate on. As I get stronger, I trust that much of my life will fall back into place again.

I will write out an affirmation that says, "I accept the way I am these days." I could even say it out loud, looking at myself in the mirror.

I am learning about decisions.

These days I'm having trouble making decisions. It's not that I'm deciding to get married or quit my job. It's making simple, everyday choices like what to do next; what to eat; do I call for support or not; do I go for a walk or stay at home and rest. I guess this is part of my mental disorder, but I feel tense and out of control when it happens.

But through my recovery group I am learning one thing that may help me get moving: a decision is not forever. I don't have to feel stuck, because I have choices. I can make one choice and later change my mind.

Today I will promptly make two decisions,
knowing I have the right to change
my mind if I want to.

I need to exercise every day.

When I had my knee operated on, they sent me home with instructions to rest my knee and to exercise it. I hardly felt like moving, let alone exercising my knee. For one thing, doing the exercises hurt and I'd had enough pain.

These days, I have a different medical problem, co-occurring disorders. When I was in treatment, I had to take part in group exercise sessions every day. At first I hated it. But as happens with me, I slowly got used to it. Eventually, to my surprise, it even felt good. I'm home now, and even though there's no one to encourage me, let alone force me, I think I'll keep up my exercise routine. I believe it will help me recover.

> *I will write down my favorite physical*
> *activity and incorporate it into*
> *my daily recovery plan.*

I am learning to handle my stress.

There are some problems in my life these days that I can't solve. (There are some I cannot even address.) It's hard to keep my mind on my job *or* my recovery from co-occurring disorders. Sometimes with the stress I think about using.

So I mentioned this to a good friend at my meeting and she offered me what works for her: breathing. When she feels stressed, she gets herself comfortable and then, breathing slowly, simply *sits still* for a while. She said it doesn't "fix" anything, but it relaxes her. It helps her gain a little more perspective and acceptance. I'm glad I have friends who can help me. I'm willing to give this a try.

Today I will take five minutes to practice
quiet breathing and letting go.

I want to feel less angry.

I feel angry much of the time these days. Nothing pleases me and everything seems to set me off. I feel tired and tense. I feel guilty and angry at myself. Is this just part of recovery?

After my support group confronted me about this, my counselor followed up with a technique to help me adjust my perspective. For example, when I feel my anger building, perhaps I can limit it by saying to myself, *I am feeling a great deal of anger lately,* or by gently reminding myself, *I am especially sensitive to change these days.* Or, instead of thinking in black and white—for instance, *My treatment program isn't working*—I might rephrase the thought as *I'm not feeling as good right now as I expected to.* I think this strategy works. I am more relaxed already.

> *I will pick one problem that is troubling me*
> *today and rephrase it to make room*
> *for some acceptance.*

I am slowing down.

I used to feel so rushed. I used to feel everything had to be done *now*. For instance, my problems must go away *now*. I want what I want *now*. Street drugs made me less anxious and frustrated, but they left me with an addiction to recover from.

Although I am in recovery from both addiction and a mental health disorder, I am still impatient at times. But it's getting better. For instance, these days I practice walking slower and driving slower. I try not to rush through a meal (especially when I am eating alone). Even the way I think is calmer. I am seeing for myself that *how* I do something—carefully, thoughtfully, completely—can often be more important than *what* I do.

> *I will take a five-minute break sometime*
> *today and practice breathing deeply*
> *and slowly.*

My health is important to me.

For a long time I couldn't let anyone know that I experience a mental disorder. It felt like a private scar. In taking medication each day, I've sometimes felt weak and vulnerable. It reminds me that I truly have a *disorder,* one that has been carefully diagnosed by a doctor, one that needs careful treatment.

But eventually I learned that I have a no-fault, biological disorder. To recover from it, I need medication, just as do patients with diabetes or heart disease. Medication helps me learn how I need to change; it helps me to make change. Taking my prescribed medication shows I have courage and commitment.

> *I will write out an affirmation that says,*
> *"I am a strong person. I am taking care*
> *of my health."*

I know now that I need people.

I used to think I didn't need people (except to sell me my drugs). But now that I'm clean and sober, I realize how lonely I've been. I realize how lost, scared, and empty I feel.

The truth is that I need people deeply. They are a part of my Higher Power. I know that I cannot recover from my co-occurring disorders on my own. Through recovery meetings, both support group and Twelve Step, I trust that I can make friends. And I trust that some of them will help me in my recovery when I need them.

> *I will tell my group how grateful I am*
> *for them and ask them for their*
> *continued support.*

I am worried about quitting my meds.

Since I've been on medication a while now, I am feeling much better. I'm stable, back at work, and feeling pretty relaxed. I attend Twelve Step meetings and therapy each week. So these days I sometimes wonder if I need meds anymore. They're expensive, inconvenient, and worst of all, they still cause me some side effects.

On the other hand, maybe I'd relapse if I stopped taking them. If I suddenly quit, perhaps I'd have a strong physiological reaction. Perhaps I'd even risk losing some of my progress. I know that recovery is my choice, but I can tell now that I'm too uncertain to make a rational decision on my own. I need professional guidance.

I will call my psychiatrist for advice
and ask my Higher Power for
wisdom and strength.

I want to be open and willing.

When my doctor gave me a (nonaddictive) medication for my anxiety, I filled it right away and took it regularly. To my surprise I still had times when I felt on edge and couldn't relax for long. Sometimes watching TV was the best I could do.

When I finally mentioned this to my therapist, he asked me how I felt about trying a relaxation technique. At first I didn't want to do anything new or different (especially since I was angry at my medication for not doing what I expected it to do). But I trusted him and began learning something else I could do to help with my symptoms. Today, I am glad I did. I'm glad I have options.

Today I will think twice before saying no
and practice being flexible.

I want to manage my urges.

I can hardly think straight. I feel sick. I feel a deep physical need to get high. It scares me.

At moments like this, I almost want to throw away all these weeks of being clean. But then I remember how difficult it has been just getting *this* far. And if I let go now, I'm afraid I'd fall into a depression again. I want recovery. With the help of my Higher Power, I can hold on. *This too shall pass.*

*I will be sure to go to a meeting or call
my sponsor when I feel urges to use.*

I want to be honest.

I am glad I'm now in the Twelve Step program, a program of honesty. Before, I couldn't admit that I had a problem with alcohol and drugs. I kept this and other secrets from others—and myself. Eventually I could no longer tolerate the lies. I realized how much I disliked myself for telling them.

Denial and lying have kept me in my disease. But when I am honest, I am free and *I like myself.* When I am honest, I truly know who I am and others know too. I can look people in the eye. Honesty gives me strength.

I will practice honesty today when
taking my daily inventory.

I can deal with my feelings of shame.

I feel bad when I think about the slips I've had. I worry that no matter what I do, I won't be able to get abstinent. It feels like I can't get this simple program. And yet I know how much I want recovery. I'm working my program as well as I can.

My sponsor reassures me that I am not a failure or a bad person—neither for having co-occurring disorders nor for having had slips. I feel relieved and happy that he still accepts me, still believes in me, and still wants to help me.

I will write out an affirmation that says,
"I am a good person in recovery and doing
the best I can." I could even say it out loud
to myself in front of a mirror.

I am learning to get the help I need.

Some days I wake up in the morning long before anyone else. My eyes open wide in the darkness and a bad dream flashes by again. But in a way, it doesn't feel like a dream. These days it feels like my life.

It's not easy to feel depressed all day long and then get little relief at night. At times I feel exhausted and hopeless. This is why I need to remind myself again and again that *I am not helpless* and that *help is available.* I can use my Twelve Step program and fellowship to help me face each day, one at a time, with courage.

Today I will promptly roll out of bed
and begin my day.

I am growing to like myself again.

Not so long ago I could hardly be bothered to crawl out of bed. When I did, I preferred to just pad about in my slippers and pajamas. I had little interest in myself or the world.

But I've come a long way in recovery. Today I popped out of bed right with the alarm. I made my bed and then put on my favorite pants and T-shirt. While brushing my hair in the mirror—surprise!—I broke into a smile. *I felt good about myself*—I felt good about the way I looked and about how I was starting my day.

Today I will practice smiling at myself in the mirror twice (even if I do not feel like it).

I want to stay on track.

For several weeks, I felt moody and irritable. Then I had a big fight with my family. It left me feeling sad and lost. I felt so bad, I was afraid I was going to get sick again.

So I promptly called my therapist, and we talked about how to prevent a relapse. In simple terms, I agreed to (*a*) be aware of my triggers and watch out for urges to use, (*b*) keep up my medication, (*c*) go to a recovery meeting regularly, and (*d*) stay in touch with my personal and professional helpers.

> *I will review my relapse prevention plan
> with my sponsor and, when needed,
> ask for additional support.*

I have friends.

I used to feel especially alone on a crowded bus or a busy sidewalk. I could hardly talk to anyone; it seemed like other people weren't part of my world. I was lonely and scared (and angry). But I didn't know what to do.

Two friends helped me when I most needed it—when I couldn't help myself. Together, they got me to a psychiatrist, who taught me about my mental disorder. It was such a relief when the medication she prescribed started working. I didn't know how troubled or isolated I really was. With medication and now therapy, I am getting connected to the world again. I feel much better. And I am very grateful to my helpers.

*I will ask a friend to call me tonight just to
see how I'm doing; then, tomorrow night,
I will call her.*

I am working a program of recovery
for two disorders.

In Twelve Step literature my three-part problem is labeled physical, emotional, and spiritual. In mental health literature, it is sometimes termed "biopsychosocial."

Whatever terms are used, the important part is that I am getting better by working a *combined* program of recovery—recovery for both my addiction and my mental disorder. Taking care of my addiction improves my mental health. Taking care of my mental health diminishes my difficulties with addiction.

I can support my recovery by taking part in a
combined Twelve Step and mental health recovery
group, such as Dual Recovery Anonymous or
Double Trouble in Recovery.

I need to focus on today.

Some days I wake up and feel bad about what I did (or didn't do) the day before—for instance, call my good friend back or take my medication. Some days I wake up and feel vaguely anxious about my future—tomorrow, for instance, can I remain abstinent and stable?

In recovery from co-occurring disorders, it helps when I forgive myself and let go of yesterday. It helps when I accept the fact that I am powerless over tomorrow. But what I *can* change and what I *am* responsible for is today, this moment. (You could say, this moment *is* my life.) And if I take care of my recovery needs right now, tomorrow will take care of itself.

I will carefully follow the activities
in today's daily recovery plan.

JULY

My problem has a name.

Before I got into recovery, I didn't know what my problem really was and I didn't know how to help myself. I was confused and I wound up running from my deep pain. The ways I tried to cope only made things worse.

I now know that I have co-occurring disorders. And to guide me I have embraced the Twelve Step program. To help recover, I will go to meetings, read the literature, and stay in touch with my sponsor and other helpers. If I do these things, I trust that I will grow stronger and my problems will weaken. I am grateful that my problem has a name because it lessens my fear and leads to a solution.

*I will carry a flash card with "Keep it simple"
on one side and the Serenity Prayer
on the other.*

I am taking care of my body.

Only now can I see how my addiction and mental disorder made it hard to take care of my body. First, I put all my energy into getting street drugs and staying high. Second, I put substances into my body that damaged it.

Free of drugs and alcohol, I am coming to care more about my physical body. I eat at regular times and I watch what I eat. I let my dog take me for a walk. When my body gets tired, I give it the extra rest it seems to need in recovery. These days I am paying attention to my body, and it feels right.

*I will incorporate my new habits
into my daily recovery plan.*

I am grateful (for what I used to take for granted).

Before I got into recovery I couldn't get what I wanted, and whatever I got wasn't enough. Life seemed a struggle and without happiness. I was caught up in feeding my addiction and avoiding my mental disorder. It felt like I was dying.

Even though I've been abstinent and stable but a few months, already I feel more relaxed, lighter. I breathe easier. I smell the air again, see the colors of the sky, and hear nature all around me. But most of all I can see that my life is more than just disorder and pain. I am alive and I am grateful for my life.

I will write down two simple things
that I am grateful for today.

My meeting keeps me out of my shell.

When I feel emotionally weak or sick and upset with myself, I don't want to see anyone and I don't want anyone to see me. I prefer to stay home and stay angry and ashamed.

I am learning, however, that it is not safe to go into this shell. If I retreat, if I stay stuck in my shame, I risk relapse. In the long run I feel better when I go to a meeting, where I feel safer with my emotions and experiences. I accept myself more when I come together with people who accept, understand, and care about me.

I will attend two meetings a week to stay
out of my shell and remain stable.

I now have choices.

Before I got into recovery I didn't really know what my problem was. I just knew I was anxious and fearful. I didn't know I had co-occurring disorders and that each disorder can affect the other. I only knew that with my moods, I kept thinking about suicide and felt I had to keep using.

Looking back I see how stuck I was. But I am no longer caught in that cycle of symptoms and intoxication. I'm mentally stable, and I no longer need street drugs to cope with my symptoms. I am learning about my problems and learning to work on solutions. I feel new freedom and strength.

I will take ten minutes today to think
about my freedom and how I can
use it in my life.

I am having a spiritual awakening.

When I first got into the program, I felt a serious burden. It was all I could do to cope with my addiction and mental health disorder. For a while, working even Step One seemed too difficult.

It's hard to describe, but these days I feel lighter. I've been working the Steps as best I can, and my effort is paying off. I still have some problems to deal with, but they no longer seem overwhelming. Nor do I feel bad about having them; they're simply part of the process I am working on. They may still hurt, but the pain is bearable because I understand and accept this process. I have faith that my problems will be resolved.

I will use Step Twelve to quietly pass along my experience, strength, and hope.

I feel stronger when I focus on the positive.

Since I have co-occurring disorders, I can easily obsess about my past, my pain, my problems. But this does not help (as I'm finding out). When I focus on my weaknesses or liabilities, I just feel weaker.

I understand that, in recovery, it is important to be aware of character defects and my behavior. But what I need to concentrate on is the present, my progress, and what I am doing to recover from my disorders. When I focus on my strengths or assets, I get what I need: more strength.

Today I will write out two affirmations
about my strengths and remind
myself of them at meals.

I am coming to accept my recovery process.

Sometimes I experience strong emotional symptoms, like suddenly becoming angry or afraid. Sometimes I have the urge to use alcohol or drugs to feel better (or at least to feel different). Even when I stay clean and sober, I can still feel uneasy at times.

These experiences upset me. Afterward I may feel worn out. But I'm learning that this is what it's like to have co-occurring disorders, even in the process of recovery. Still I am grateful to know something about my disorders and grateful to be learning about the many ways I can deal with them—through counseling, Twelve Step meetings or other support groups, sponsors or friends, and acceptance.

I will write down this sentence in my journal:
"I accept the way I am and my process of recovery."
I could even say it out loud to someone
who understands me.

I am learning about side effects.

I don't understand—I didn't feel this tired *before* I started taking my prescribed medication. I feel jittery and I'm often thirsty. What's especially hard is that with these changes I often feel irritable.

When I mentioned this medication problem to my doctor, whom I trust, she helped me understand it. I learned that (*a*) by itself, recovering from co-occurring disorders takes a lot of energy; (*b*) I am still getting over the effects of street drugs in my body; and (*c*) my medication may well cause some jitteriness and thirstiness—it's a common complaint. Knowing all this helps me relax with these changes and discomforts.

To help adjust to the side effects of my medication,
I will rest when I need it, practice a relaxation
exercise, drink fluids, and avoid caffeine,
especially before bed.

I can enjoy each day.

When I was using and having serious symptoms, my life was troubled and chaotic. Each day was much like the last (some just held less distress than others). I just wanted to forget them.

But in recovery I experience my life differently. Now that I am free of mood-altering drugs and stable on psychiatric medication, the chaos is gone. I no longer want to forget my days. I am learning how to feel useful and enjoy each day once again. As I take part in my recovery activities, I feel more connected to my life and the world around me.

Today I will take a risk and do something new.

I will not play doctor.

I tried hanging on to control. I thought I could manage my symptoms on my own with street drugs. It didn't work. After a long time and a lot of painful disruption in my life, I finally acknowledged just how out of control I was.

I know now that I have two disorders and that I am not the doctor. To deal with my addiction and mental health disorder, I need the help of professionals and others who have recovery. Although it is still hard for me to trust people, I hit bottom trying to do it all on my own. I want to recover and I will accept the help I need.

When I need help, I will contact one of my helpers.
If I'm having a problem with my medication,
I will call my doctor right away.

I know that abstinence is critical to my recovery.

When I used alcohol and drugs, I felt as though I was rejecting myself and even rejecting others who wanted to help me. Sometimes I felt weak and out of control because I knew I was hurting myself and couldn't seem to stop.

But when I'm abstinent from alcohol and drugs, I still feel stress. At times I get irritable and anxious and don't sleep well. At times I think about using again. It's a struggle. But at least when I'm abstinent, I don't have to feel guilty or ashamed. I feel clearer about my recovery from co-occurring disorders. I know I'm doing the right thing. And the struggle is worth it.

When I feel cravings, I will promptly apply the tools of my program to deal with them.

I want to show my gratitude with service.

Not long ago it was all I could do to get out of bed. I was angry at the world for my co-occurring disorders. Everything seemed to be going wrong. I was grateful to no one and nothing.

Since getting into the Twelve Step program, however, I am doing and feeling much better. Slowly my program has led me to acceptance and abstinence. It has even helped me to get stable in my mental health. I feel such fullness and gratitude these days that I want to share it. I want to give back some of what I've been given. I want to help others feel better too.

I will express my gratitude for the program
and my home group and humbly offer
to be of service.

I am getting honest.

I couldn't face my co-occurring disorders at first; the diagnosis was too confusing and threatening. I denied it to myself and to others. For example, I kept using street drugs, even when I was first in treatment, to reduce the symptoms of my mental health disorder.

But having made a commitment to recovery, I am coming to see how much it can help when I admit my weaknesses, my liabilities, to myself. It leaves me open to change. And when I tell another person about these liabilities, I find out that I am still OK, that I'm not a bad person after all. When I am honest and open, I no longer feel so alone. Instead, I feel forgiven and accepted.

I will use my journal and write down two secrets about myself that I haven't told anyone yet.

I now have a spiritual life, thanks to my disorders.

Had I been given a choice about experiencing addiction and mental disorder, no doubt I would have declined. It is painful even to think about what I've gone through to reach this stage in recovery.

But through my no-fault disorders (and because I am accepting them more and more), two wonderful changes are in process: (*a*) As I begin to care for my own physical and emotional needs in a healthy way, I find myself caring more about other people, and (*b*) I am developing a relationship with a Higher Power and becoming a more spiritual person. For these surprising new changes, I am profoundly grateful.

> *Today I will compose a prayer or draw
> a picture that acknowledges my process
> and progress in recovery.*

I will be abstinent today.

It used to be that my most important goal each day was to cope with the pain of my co-occurring disorders. I did it mostly by using alcohol and drugs. Mostly it didn't work.

Today, that "solution" seems ironic. Because in recovery, the way I stop the pain is to *not* use substances. Today, *abstinence* is my most important goal. And I know I can do it. I have done it before. I have several tools to work with, especially meetings, the telephone, and my sponsor. With the help of my Higher Power, today I will be gratefully, humbly abstinent.

Today I will meditate on the value of
abstinence in my recovery and
check in with my sponsor.

I am looking forward to returning to work.

Because of my co-occurring disorders, for now I can't return to work. My addiction fueled my mental health symptoms, which scared me into further use of drugs. I spiraled deeper into disorder and needed a medical leave from work to get stable, both physically and mentally.

To my surprise, not working has been hard. I miss having a place to go during the day and being with people I enjoy. In particular, I miss the feeling of making a contribution. But with the help of my Higher Power, I plan to return to work soon.

*I will pick up an extra recovery meeting
and work on today's job: my recovery.*

I need help with my cravings.

I don't like this state I'm in. All I can think about right now is using. And I'm tired of feeling scared and anxious. I just want some relief. At times like this, I don't care if it's only temporary: changing my mood is all that matters.

Being hooked like this is painful, especially since the relief I get from drugs and alcohol *doesn't* last—I *know* that. My cravings just come back, sometimes stronger than before. So why does a part of me still believe in this lie? I read somewhere that this lie is part of the disease. I'm still confused. But I want to be clean and sober. I want to change my thinking and my behavior. I want to feel better.

My sponsor said I could call her
anytime. I will pick up the phone
now and ask for her help.

I need to remember HALT.

Suddenly I feel very irritated. Why? I don't know. I know I'm upset, but I don't know what to do. I feel out of control. I feel like using. This has happened before and I don't know what's going on.

When I have these sudden changes in mood, I need to recall the tried and true slogan, HALT (Hungry, Angry, Lonely, Tired). Several times I've heard about this tool for staying in touch with four important feelings. When I sense a change in mood, which often happens to me these days, I need to ask myself whether I am feeling especially hungry, angry, lonely, or tired. If I know what I'm feeling, I feel less out of control, and I can figure out what to do next—even if it's nothing.

I will make a HALT flash card and
carry it with me as a reminder.

I am working to keep my faith.

I've been taking my prescribed medication and going to support meetings long enough to feel better. I do feel better, but I still have strong symptoms from time to time. Now my doctor wants me to try another medication—with, of course, a new regimen and new side effects. These days I feel very weary. At times I feel lost.

And yet I know I am not alone. I have a home. I have my recovery program and for that I am grateful. It reminds me that I didn't cause these disorders and I can't cure them. It encourages me to keep doing the good things I've been doing. My Higher Power and my program have brought me this far; I trust that they will carry me further.

*I will list two improvements I've made
in recovery and ask my sponsor for
support with my meds.*

I can recover from a relapse.

It scares me to think back over the past few weeks. The symptoms of my mental disorder returned—I felt lost and I lost control. I even had a lapse with my addiction.

The message I take from this, however, is that I have two disorders that can affect one another sharply. I need to work a recovery program for both of them at the same time. (And even then the biological part of my mental disorder could flare up.) Although I can't get back these recent weeks of disorder, I can decide to take better care of myself. For starters, I will make today as good as it can be.

> *I will look at my relapse triggers for both*
> *my addiction and my mental disorder*
> *and adjust my relapse plan as necessary.*

I am glad that I have accepted help.

Before I hit bottom, I didn't know I needed help with my drug-using behavior. After I hit bottom and got an assessment, I didn't want any help. I didn't want to deal with my addiction, I denied my mental health problems, and I wanted to be left alone.

In recovery from co-occurring disorders, I now see how much I needed help and how much help I can use. My sponsor supports my spiritual and emotional growth. My treatment team manages my mental disorder. Instead of feeling lost or friendless, I feel understood and cared for. And I am grateful.

I will meditate on the two ways I have
changed the most since I accepted help
for my co-occurring disorders.

My Twelve Step group is a home.

When I was a child growing up, there was both addiction and mental disorder in my family. In my house there was too much fear, chaos, and neglect. There was too little "home" in my house when I was growing up.

As an adult, I'm working through my own addiction and mental disorder. But now I've found a home that always offers me safety, stability, and nurturing: my Twelve Step group. Where else am I always welcomed, whether happy or sad? Listened to, whether foolish or wise? Who else offers me help without getting in my way? Cares about my successes *and* my failures? Where else can I be fully myself and yet be respected? This is why I call it home.

> *I will meditate on my experience of home—*
> *what I missed, what I am now getting,*
> *what else I want.*

I am learning how to relax.

Some days I can't think with all the noises and voices around me. I want it all to stop. Some days I feel trapped.

At times like these it helps me to keep in mind that, first of all, it's OK to be sensitive to noise (no matter what others might say). Second, I can cope. One skill I need to remember is to get comfortable and take a deep breath to the count of four—one, two, three, four—and then breathe out to the count of four—one, two, three, four. And then do this exercise for four minutes. I am finding out that when I breathe slowly, I tend to relax. I will be OK.

> *I will practice my breathing exercises*
> *four times today: four counts in,*
> *four out, for four minutes.*

I am getting to know myself.

Before I got into recovery for my co-occurring disorders, I usually didn't know what I was feeling. Often I didn't know what I wanted—except to avoid the pain of my mental health disorder. I couldn't think things through, I just reacted impulsively. I was running away and running on automatic.

Now that I'm sober and stable, I am slowing down. My thinking is clearer and I'm recognizing more of my feelings (it's scary at times). In my support group, I have a safe place to find out what I want. In short, I am learning about myself through others who share my problems. Despite what I used to believe, I see that I am not alone and I am not a bad person.

I will write out a description of two things
I've learned about myself this week.

I am becoming a spiritual person.

"Spiritual" used to mean church or religion to me—both of which I rejected. In a way I was my own Higher Power and I tried to handle all my problems on my own. As a result, I often felt alone, insecure, and afraid.

Now that I am in recovery for co-occurring disorders, I am learning little by little the larger meaning of the word *spiritual*. Most important, it means I am not alone, I have a Higher Power, one who cares about me. When I let my Higher Power help, I feel more confidence and courage. I worry less about what will happen tomorrow and try to be grateful for today.

> *When I wake up in the morning,*
> *I will practice welcoming the day.*

I know what to do when I feel overwhelmed.

Sometimes it feels overwhelming to try to stay off alcohol and drugs *and* get a grip on my mental disorder. I feel so unsure of anything. So much is changing—my habits, thinking, friends, lifestyle. I feel off-balance and afraid.

Recovering from co-occurring disorders is work. But I have a feeling that if I can just keep putting one foot in front of the other, I will get better. (And I don't have to do the work all on my own or all at once.) I can't predict how my life will change in recovery. But I trust that it will be better. And I trust that in this process, I am becoming a happier and healthier person.

> *When I feel overwhelmed, I will pray*
> *to my Higher Power for strength and*
> *call a supportive friend.*

I need courage to change.

After doing Steps Four and Five in my recovery program, I'm spiritually and emotionally tired. (They were especially hard to do given the shame and guilt I have felt in my depression.) I don't much feel like making any more changes in Steps Six and Seven. Haven't I made enough changes by getting stable and abstinent?

And yet, how can I stop now? As I'm learning in the program, I work Steps Four and Five so I'm free to make these changes in myself. I know it will not be easy, but I need to begin to let go of the parts of my personality that cause me trouble—the parts that, in recovery, no longer help. I need to *become open* to change in Step Six and then *invite* change in Step Seven. With strength from my Higher Power, I can do this much and trust the results.

Today I will pray for the courage to allow myself to be changed through my Higher Power.

I want to stop worrying.

I'm coming to terms with the fact that I think too much or, more accurately, worry too much. I'd rather stop. I can see now that it doesn't do me much good. In fact, the more I think (more like *obsess*), the more troubled and stuck I get, and the less I can do about it.

And the less I can do, the less I can change. But to recover, *I need to change.* It may be gradual, but to recover from my mental health and substance use disorders, I need to change both the way I think and my lifestyle. "Obsessing myself" into paralysis will not help.

For five minutes today I will try to
simply sit, breathe deeply, and not think
(what you might call "meditate").

It's OK for me to have fun again.

Recovering from a drug addiction and a mental health disorder is a lot of work. Every week I see my therapist and attend two recovery meetings. Slowly I am changing my life. Recovery is a long-term process, but it is not the whole of my life. In fact recovery, too, calls for balance.

The other day I got inspired to hop on my dusty bike and take a ride around my neighborhood. I felt the speed and the wind and the freedom. Suddenly I realized *I was smiling.* I was having fun! I want more!

Today I will set aside at least
ten minutes to do something fun.

I need to "Keep it simple."

I am slowly learning about my two chronic disorders—addiction and a mental health disorder—and how to recover from them. Basically, I must take care of my emotional problem to make sure it doesn't stir up my drug problem, and I must take care of my drug problem to make sure it doesn't stir up my emotional problem.

These days I feel deeply grateful for the Twelve Step fellowship, one simple program that can help me with two mutually complicating disorders. I have faith (and growing confidence) that if I follow my doctor's recommendations, work my Twelve Step program, and learn more about recovery from co-occurring disorders, I will recover.

I will ask my Higher Power to help me
keep my simple and basic program
of recovery strong.

AUGUST

I acknowledge the benefits of treatment.

When I was in treatment, I felt scared and ashamed at first. I didn't know anyone. I didn't trust anyone. I didn't know what would happen. I was angry and exhausted.

But it became clear that treatment was a good place to be with my co-occurring disorders after all. Eventually I felt more relaxed, safer, understood. I acknowledged that I needed to be there (for months I'd just kept relapsing). While it wasn't easy adjusting to new faces, new routines, and new ideas, I was tired of suffering. Eventually I let go of my fears and found the relief and the freedom of recovery.

*I will continue to pray the Serenity Prayer
and pray to be open to change.*

I want to trust people more.

My therapist wants me to join a support group. He wants me to work on trust. But it's hard for me to trust other people (even my therapist). I feel safer when I rely on myself (although that hasn't always worked). I am afraid to trust because I'm afraid I'll get hurt, betrayed, or abandoned like so many times before. How could I ever take part in a group?

And yet maybe now is a good time to take a chance. I am exhausted from trying to handle my mental health and substance use problems on my own for so long. And deep down, there is loneliness, there is a part of me that truly wants to be around people more. With the support of my therapist, I will give group therapy a chance.

*Today I will practice trusting by taking
a small risk with a safe person.*

I am reclaiming my life.

My life has been out of control for a long time now due to my addiction and mental health disorder. First the addiction seemed in control, then the mental disorder. Together, the two proved more than I could handle on my own.

After struggling to get abstinent and then get stable on medication, and after several months in both a Twelve Step group and a support group, I am beginning to reclaim my life. As I take responsibility for my disorders, I am finding out where I was and exploring where I want to go. Each day I do the best I can. I am recovering.

Today I will draw a picture or write about
the way I want my future to look.

My past is no longer my present.

Growing up, I was abandoned physically and emotionally—and felt lost. As an adult, I experience addiction and mental disorder—and have felt a victim. While I can't change my past, I need to understand it and accept it so I am better able to deal with my present.

In recovery I do this in two ways. First, I take part in the Twelve Step fellowship for recovery—a stable, nurturing, spiritual community. Second, I take part in therapy—a safe, educational, and healing community. With the help of these two programs, I am developing a new outlook: *I am no longer a victim.* I take care of myself—physically, emotionally, and spiritually—and I am taken care of.

I will meditate on how my past affects my present
and how taking care of myself in the present
can help me accept my past.

I am slowly embracing the truth.

When I was having symptoms of my mental disorder, they scared me. I wouldn't talk about them with anyone. I didn't think I'd be accepted or understood. And when I was getting high all the time, I'd deny it. Again, my experience scared me. I felt guilty, ashamed, afraid of punishment, and afraid of losing my source of relief.

In recovery, I have a different idea about being honest and open. I am learning that when I speak the truth, people understand me better. When I say what I'm thinking or feeling, they have a connection to me. When they know what's troubling me, chances are they can help.

I will write down two ways in which getting honest has helped me begin to recover.

I want to make today a day of recovery.

A lot of time has passed with my co-occurring disorders. It feels like I've lost years of my life. First, the mental health problem and then the using, when everything got much worse.

But I am coming around. I'm stable and I haven't used drugs now for quite a while. I feel like I've finally come to rest after a long, uncontrolled slide. Now I need to let go of my past—I can't get it back—and concentrate on today. I only get a day at a time. I want to make the most of each one.

I will meditate on what I need to do today
to make it a day of recovery.

I have strength and patience.

When I was at bottom with my co-occurring disorders, I could hardly get out of bed or stop crying. I could hardly eat or stop obsessing. I was desperate. I was afraid that I might never find relief. Finally I got evaluated by a psychiatrist who prescribed therapy and a psychiatric medication. She warned me that it would take a couple of weeks for the medicine to become effective. It felt like forever.

But with the help of my Higher Power and my sponsor, I managed to hang on until the medication could take effect. And through the process, I learned something very important about myself: I have more strength and patience than I ever knew. I am strong enough to allow time to help me heal.

*In my journal I will describe two ways
I am strong or patient.*

I need to let go of temporary losses.

I make my favorite meal and it doesn't satisfy me. I go out to eat and nothing on the menu interests me. I feel hungry but can't eat. There are times these days when I feel angry with my co-occurring disorders; I can't enjoy something that has given me pleasure in the past. Sometimes it feels like there is little left in my day to look forward to. (And then I feel more like using.)

But to avoid a slip, I need to keep in mind that recovery involves upset and change—letting go of old ways, slowly learning new ones. And letting go includes losses—even temporary ones, like my favorite foods. In the meantime, I might discover some delicious *new* food.

> *I will come up with two foods and two*
> *activities that I still enjoy these days,*
> *despite my disorders.*

I want to stop acting out.

I had been sober and stable for a while and it felt great. But then recently I had a lapse. Almost before I was aware of it, almost without thinking, I became very upset and then acted out.

I was nervous but I brought this up at my group anyway. In the discussion, I learned that urges usually weaken in just a few minutes. (Could I practice waiting them out? Could I learn a relaxation technique?) I also learned that to avoid lapses that can turn into slips, to avoid overreacting, it helps to know what I am feeling at any given time and to know what pushes my buttons.

*At some point today I will take a few
minutes to get relaxed and find out
what I am feeling.*

I want to face my anxieties.

I used to always think something bad was going to happen. It was less a thought than a general feeling. I wasn't aware of it all of the time—but it was there. I wanted to prevent it, but I didn't know how. I didn't really know what to prevent. Worrying like that made it harder for me to relax, harder for me to get anything done.

One day I finally got tired of worrying so much, realized I needed help, and contacted my counselor. First, she reassured me that many folks in recovery from addiction experience anxiety. She said it might subside over time, but that I could talk with a psychiatrist if I wanted to. Then she taught me a helpful relaxation exercise that I could practice at home, whether I consulted a doctor or not. Just acknowledging my anxiety helped me feel better that day—just as it does today.

I will make a list of what I am worried about today and trust that I can get help.

I can read to help myself recover.

When I got into my Twelve Step program, I was told that to recover from addiction, it was important to go to meetings regularly and read the Big Book—the textbook for AA. I got to the meetings, but with my mental disorder I couldn't concentrate enough to read, at least at first. But with the help of my psychiatrist, eventually I was able to start using the program literature as a recovery tool.

I never used to read a lot, but reading the literature these days is worth it. As suggested, reading helps me accept my addiction (and my mental disorder). It also teaches me ways to recover, ways to feel relief. I read a little each day and feel connected to others in recovery. In reading I am developing a *good* habit.

*I will spend ten minutes today
reading recovery materials.*

My sponsor still cares about me.

First I had a slip with my addiction, which then led to a setback with my mental disorder. I'm missing work these days and my family is angry. I don't think they understand my disorders very well or know what to do. (Sometimes I feel the same way.) I know they don't like what is happening, and right now I don't think they like *me.* (I don't like myself a lot either.)

Maybe this is the way it has to be for a while. It doesn't feel good, but at least I still have my sponsor to talk with. I couldn't handle all this alone. He listens to me; he does not judge; he tells me he cares (and I feel it). *This* is what I need—a person I can go to at any time for support, no matter what happens. And for this gift I am very grateful.

When I check in with my sponsor today,
I will thank him for all his support.

I can love myself.

When I remember all the times I got high, all the junk I ate, all the sleep I lost, all the anger I kept inside (and the times I hurt myself through a rage turned inward), I realize that I have not loved myself much. It scares me to look back and imagine where I was headed.

But slowly through recovery, I have begun to turn my life around, and today I am doing things differently. I am clean and sober, eating better on a regular schedule, and getting the rest I need. I'm even taking medication to help me with the symptoms of my mental health disorder. I feel shy saying it (I guess it's just not familiar), but I care about myself today and I truly want to be healthy.

Today I will look at myself in the mirror
and say "I love you"—or at the very least,
"I'm worth caring about."

I need to make a list of my assets.

I keep seeing myself as a person whose life revolves around having a mental health disorder and a substance use disorder. I feel as though I'm just a patient who can't do anything but be sick and keep trying to get well, to recover.

Perhaps it would help if I did a kind of Fourth Step inventory on this question. I could write out a list of my assets—my personal qualities, abilities, accomplishments, and interests. Then when I feel bad about the time and effort that my two disorders demand, I can remind myself of the *whole* truth: I am a competent, valuable person who is in recovery from co-occurring disorders.

Today I will label a sheet of paper "Assets"
and start out the list with two of my
most helpful ones.

I help myself when I help others.

I was feeling worse than I had in a long time. I felt I could do nothing right. All I wanted to do was give up and get high. So when my sponsor first suggested it, I didn't understand how doing a helpful deed for someone could possibly lighten my mood.

But because I trusted my sponsor, I gathered up what strength I had and gave it a try. She was right—an important spiritual surprise. By doing a favor for someone else, I felt better about myself—even in the midst of my own distress. I saw that I have strength in reserve and that I am a worthwhile person. I recognized that other people have needs too—needs that I can help with. When I help others, even for just a little while, I am less caught up in myself.

Today I will do something kind
for someone (anonymously).

I want courage and honesty.

Sometimes I don't want to go to my meeting. I especially didn't want to after I had a slip and had to admit that I wasn't clean or sober. I felt I'd let myself down (or somehow had let down the group). I felt guilty, ashamed.

I've since learned that the members of my Twelve Step group will still accept me and help me—if I ask. What I have been learning in the program is how important honesty is to recovery. (I have lied to myself long enough.) To get help, I need to be open about my problems and my behavior with the people who can help me. It's the only way I can handle my addiction (as well as my mental disorder). When things are going well, it's easy for me to go to meetings. When I'm unsure about my sobriety or my recovery, it takes courage.

I will pray for courage and use my
daily Step Ten inventory to stay
honest with myself.

I gain strength and serenity in the program.

Of late my life is troubled. My mind is plagued, my body abused, my spirit downcast. My addiction ignites the depression, which fans the addiction. The cycle is strong.

But the cycle is weakening. As I continue to practice my Twelve Step program, devoting time to it each day, I feel stronger and less troubled. By attending meetings each week and listening carefully to fellow members— my strong and humble teachers—I am coming to accept myself *as I am, with all my problems.*

To help myself by helping others,
I will offer to do service for my group.

I am not a bad person.

When I think about making an Eighth Step list of people I have harmed, I feel guilty and shameful. I get a knot in my stomach and start to feel down.

But there is that hopeful, spiritual part of me that knows I'm not a bad person, even though I've hurt people. What is true is that I have two no-fault disorders, and that particularly when using, I did some things I feel bad about and would not do again. What's also true is that this is *just* a list (no actions are needed yet), it is my list (no one need see it), and I can take my time. It helps when I keep in mind that I am a different person today, one with awareness, strength, and purpose.

Today I will make a list of the people
I care about and do an act of kindness
for one of them.

I can accept how I feel right now.

I can't change my mood just because I don't like feeling angry, sad, or fatigued. It's not comfortable, but this is just the way I feel right now. True, at times there are some things I can do about my mood, but for the most part, I just have to go with it. Sometimes, it changes on its own. Sometimes it lingers painfully.

My job, however, is to *accept* my emotion or mood (even when others around me don't). I need to be with it, let it be, not act out. Once I accept it, then I'll know what to do about it (if anything).

I will call a friend to talk about
what I am feeling.

I am finding forgiveness.

Now that I'm in recovery for co-occurring disorders, I am looking at my life more closely—and I can see more of the mistakes I've made. There are lots of smaller ones and some big ones too. At times, it feels overwhelming. At times, I feel deeply discouraged.

But it usually helps when I take the time to settle down and remember some points I've learned in the program. In recovery it is not uncommon to feel bad about past behavior. Everybody makes mistakes; I am beginning to learn from mine (and go on to explore who I am and what I want). Finally, even with my faults, I am accepted.

> *I will write out an affirmation that says,*
> *"I accept myself—faults and all."*

I have a new perspective.

I have been working on my recovery from co-occurring disorders for a while now. I have insight into where I've come from, where I want to go, and what I need to do to get there. In brief, I have some perspective.

To me, "perspective" means I don't have to fix everything right now. I don't finish working the Twelve Steps in twelve weeks. There are no grades and no graduating classes in recovery. Perspective also suggests balance. For example, although I experience two chronic disorders—addiction and a mental health disorder—the disorders do not define me. I am, first of all, a human being.

To help me keep my perspective, I will
read the comics in today's paper.

I want to be supportive.

I work Step Twelve to the best of my ability. But sometimes when a friend from group calls me for support, I don't feel like talking. Sometimes I'm simply tired. At other times, my friend may not seem to understand his problem or how to help himself, or perhaps he doesn't seem to listen or appreciate what I have to offer. Then again, maybe he expects too much of me.

I know my reactions are valid and honest, but I need to step back from them a bit. It will help if I remember that (*a*) being asked for help is a gift; (*b*) at times, I am difficult to help too; (*c*) it's OK to set boundaries; and (*d*) *simply being present* to another's pain is a loving, transforming experience.

*I will ask my Higher Power
for strength to carry the message
with patience and love.*

I can put up with some side effects.

I knew I didn't want to take psychiatric medication. I knew there would be problems. That's why I hesitated at first—and I was right. Now I feel edgy and tired out much of the time. I'm often thirsty. And to top it off, my sex drive is diminished. I don't like trading in one sort of problem for another.

On the other hand, the medication *is* helping to reduce my symptoms. I don't feel as sad and I'm sleeping better. Most of the day I can function pretty well. I guess relief from my major symptoms is worth putting up with some side effects.

*I will follow my medication regimen carefully
and call my doctor with any questions.*

My life isn't easy, but it's mine and it's real.

For quite some time, my life consisted of fighting my mental disorder, mainly by getting high. But in trying to control the emotional—almost physical—pain, I was losing control of my life. I was caught in a web.

These days it can still be a struggle—stress, setbacks, holding down a job—but now I have the right tools and I know where I am: I'm abstinent and stable. I am doing the work I need to do—counseling, Twelve Step meetings—and I'm on the right path.

Today I will pray for continued strength and the willingness to trust my Higher Power with my future.

I need to eat right to stay in recovery.

I used to eat whatever was easy to get—especially junk food—as long as I got full (sometimes too full). Other times I'd lose my appetite and skip meals. It all depended on my mood and on whether I was intoxicated.

Now that I'm in recovery for co-occurring disorders, I feel differently about what and how I eat. I now recognize how important it is to eat a healthy diet to stay strong, both physically and mentally (these are not separate). Moreover, instead of abusing my body or ignoring it like I did before, in recovery I want to help it.

I will list three foods I want to
eat more of these days.

I need to be gentle with myself.

As I am seeing my mental health disorder and addiction more and more clearly, I am coming to see just how they have affected my life. Sometimes I feel afraid and ashamed and guilty and overwhelmed. Sometimes I don't like the way I am or what I've done.

At times like these, it usually helps when I promptly share my struggle with my support person. He reassures me that my feelings are not unusual. Then he reminds me to keep thinking about three things: (*a*) being gentle with myself as my awareness deepens, (*b*) respecting myself for the courage and strength I have already shown, and (*c*) forgiving myself. When I think of his helpful words and his acceptance of me, I can better accept myself and move through this difficult stage.

I will write down one positive thing
I have done today and then add
one reason I like myself.

I am slowly accepting my feelings.

I was afraid to talk to anyone about my feelings. They were so powerful and frightening at times. When I did tell people what I was feeling, often they didn't understand. Some even got angry with me. Eventually I kept them to myself. But by not letting my feelings out—and using drugs in part to avoid them—I slowly developed a second disorder: drug addiction.

In recovery, I am learning a lot about feelings and what to do with them. For instance, a feeling won't kill me. It's OK to have feelings (*all* of them), and it helps to let them out (without harming myself or others). So now, at group I practice talking about my feelings. At home I practice sharing with my support person on the phone. I even write about my feelings sometimes in a journal. I am learning to make them my friends.

*I will ask myself what I am feeling right now—
and then briefly write about these
feelings in my journal.*

I feel better today.

It used to be that each day was just as dull or unhappy as the one before it. I kept doing the same things that kept me down—using street drugs, ignoring my prescribed medication, and ignoring the professional help that was offered me. The week I hit bottom, each day was worse than the one before.

But now it feels like I'm finally into recovery. I've been drug-free for several weeks and attending my group. Last night I took my meds on time and went to sleep at a reasonable hour. Today I woke up in a good mood, did my daily recovery activities, and then wrote a while in my journal. I even took a risk: I called a family member just to talk. It was good to hear his voice (I think he accepts me more these days). Things are looking up.

Today I will give myself a healthful reward for my commitment to recovery.

• AUGUST 29 •

I know what to do if I have a setback.

Recently I had a slip with my addiction. My sponsor quickly helped me get back on track. Then I asked myself, *What would happen if I had a setback with my mental disorder? Would that be a different matter to deal with?* Even though I'm stable on medication, I understand that it could still happen.

So I wound up asking a friend from my support group if she would be willing to watch out for me, just as my sponsor does. She said yes. Then we agreed on what steps should be taken if I had a setback and couldn't take care of myself. Even though I don't expect a problem, I feel better now that I have a good plan in place.

I will write down my important setback/relapse plans—just in case.

I need to keep talking.

I feel sad, sometimes even helpless these days. Sometimes I end up crying at work and then I feel worse—fragile, out of control. Even if I tried to talk about my fears and feelings, I don't think anyone would understand.

Or would they? Am I just feeling sorry for myself? When I start feeling this bad, it's tough for me to get past my shame and fear of rejection. But if I don't try, I start to isolate myself and that only makes matters worse. Perhaps I really do need to talk. I need to keep moving through the pain.

I will call a caring friend to listen to me.
If need be, I can begin the conversation
by stating the truth: it's hard for me
to be open about my feelings.

I am learning to say yes.

Living with both addiction and mental disorder, I see that I have many issues to deal with. When things don't go my way or when I don't get my needs met, I quickly feel hurt, frustrated, angry. Sometimes I even feel mistreated. Sometimes I ask, Why me?

But as I grow in my recovery from co-occurring disorders, I am slowly learning acceptance, to say yes. I am learning to accept who I am and what happens to me—to say yes to it—whether to stress, symptoms, or setbacks. When I say yes, *I let go*—and the moment I let go, I am stronger.

I will write out a reminder to myself that reads,
"Yes. This is the way it is. I will be OK."

SEPTEMBER

I can accept my shortcomings.

It hurt to become so aware of my shortcomings through Step Four. I did feel better—less guilty and shameful—when I admitted them to another person in Step Five. But what I really wanted was to get rid of them quickly and completely.

However, I am slowly coming to see that my shortcomings are not all bad. Some were useful to me at one time—and some are now blocking my spiritual progress. Only my Higher Power knows which are which. What I need to do is to work Steps Six and Seven by accepting myself, becoming open to change, and by letting my Higher Power decide which shortcomings to remove and when to remove them.

I will pray the Serenity Prayer and pray
to follow the will of my Higher Power.

I am learning not to reject myself for mistakes.

I had a slip in my recovery from addiction. I felt sorry and ashamed. I felt like a failure—unworthy of help, unworthy of recovery.

Fortunately, I remembered to get ahold of my sponsor. I told her what I'd done and how I felt about myself. She listened to me calmly, carefully. When she spoke, she offered support without judging. Soon I felt lighter, no longer so alone: I felt accepted. It only took one other person to let me know that, even though I'd had a slip, *I was still OK.* I was not rejected—even though I'd rejected myself. Perhaps now I can begin to forgive myself.

I will talk about my mistakes, and
forgiving myself, with my group.

I feel better this month.

Last month I didn't want to accept addiction on *top* of my mental health disorder. I wanted to quit taking my prescribed medication, and I thought about skipping my Step meetings. I even thought about having a drink—just one. It was a period of anger, conflict, and denial.

But I worked through it with the support of my therapist, and now I'm working hard again on my recovery from both of my disorders. Things are looking up. I got my meds adjusted so I am not as tired all the time, and I asked a friend in my home group to be my sponsor and she said yes. I'm feeling better about myself these days. I admit that I have two problems, and I am glad that I am dealing with them, little by little.

Today I will start keeping a list of
any changes I make as I recover.

I want to live.

I am slowly changing my life. I no longer use street drugs. I have given up my using friends. I have stopped trying to manage the symptoms of my mental disorder by self-medicating with alcohol and drugs. I admit my serious problem: co-occurring disorders.

These days I wake up feeling clearheaded. I am learning about my disorders and coming to accept them. My new recovering friends care about me more than my old using ones. More and more I am facing the world and taking care of myself the best I can. I have developed some strength and courage. I truly want to live.

Today I will feel my strength
and take a healthy risk.

I am learning to live with my feelings.

In one way, using alcohol and drugs was exciting. I could just take a drink or pop a pill to change my mood (even if it lasted only a short time). I felt I had some control and power.

But now that I am in recovery, I use no alcohol or street drugs. With nothing to alter my mood, I am more aware of how I am feeling at any time. Sometimes there's pain, sometimes boredom. (There's certainly less control.) And more and more, there's even some joy. In short, I am slowly learning to accept and to live with my feelings. I believe that the reward of long-term recovery is worth it.

I will pray for strength to handle my feelings
(and call for support as needed).

I need to practice letting go.

Before recovery I worried about losing my job. My symptoms were getting worse, and it was getting harder to go to work and be productive. Briefly I tried to keep it together through willpower. Then I tried medicating my symptoms with alcohol and drugs. But in the long run, they didn't help either. I simply developed an addiction on top of my mental disorder.

Now I'm finally accepting help with my co-occurring disorders through a therapist and a Twelve Step program. But at times I *still* worry about losing my job. Fortunately, these days I can take a spiritual approach to my fears. Less and less do I have to "fix" them. Instead, for instance, I can work Step Three again and practice letting go. If I keep up my medication, stay sober, and turn my worry over to my Higher Power—if I do what I can do for myself today—perhaps my job will take care of itself.

I will read about Step Three in the
Big Book today and be sure to go to
an extra meeting this week.

I am coming to believe.

It has not been easy for me to believe in a Higher Power. I grew up with no one to trust. When I hit bottom with addiction and mental disorder—that is, when street drugs made the mental health symptoms worse—I felt hopeless and helpless, and realized I had nowhere to turn.

But eventually I found a Higher Power in the spiritual fellowship of recovery. Slowly I am learning to *talk* to my Higher Power, to pray. Slowly I am learning to *listen* to my Higher Power, to meditate. These days I feel closest to my Higher Power at meetings, where I witness the other members' strength and feel their hope.

Today I will tell my Higher Power
about one problem I need help with.

*I need to take on more responsibility
for my recovery.*

Because I have co-occurring disorders, I need help from different helping professionals. I need to learn to trust them, but I also need to listen to myself.

When I first got help for my problems, I was treated for depression, then addiction, then depression again. Nobody really knew what was going on with me or how best to help me. Eventually I realized something: I needed to assume more responsibility for my recovery. With any treatment, I need to keep talking about what is—and what is not—working for me. I am the only one who really knows what I am feeling. When I speak up, I am taking care of myself.

*At some point in my day, I will take a
quiet moment to find out how I am feeling.*

I want to settle down.

I am sad and anxious and angry about this mental disorder I've got. It's hard to think straight. I feel confused. I feel like I'm floundering.

Yet those who support me don't seem worried. What I am picking up is that these problems are not unusual in recovery from co-occurring disorders. I've started a new medication, and I gather that in a couple of weeks, as it takes effect, I'll be able to settle down, not think so hard or worry so much. I wish things were better right now, but it seems I need to cope a while longer. With the help of my Higher Power, I will manage.

*Today I will take two walks and
call two friends on the phone.*

I am beginning to lighten up.

Before I got help for my addiction and depression, I was typically serious and sad. I spent little time with other people and spoke little. Laughing didn't feel natural; eventually my smile went away.

Even in recovery it's still hard to come out of my shell, but the truth is, I am worn out from all this gravity and intensity. It's a good thing too. I believe I'm finally gaining some perspective—maybe even a sense of humor. Perhaps I'm getting ready to let go of some pain. I hope so. It would be a welcome relief.

I will watch a favorite comedy movie
and see how hard I have to work
not to laugh at least once.

I am coming out of hiding.

I used to believe that given a chance, most people would only hurt me or use me. I could not trust them. I could not ask anything of them. So I kept to myself. Being alone was one way I could feel safe.

But these days I am learning that being alone and afraid and untrusting won't help me recover from my co-occurring disorders. What *does* help, among other things, is when my counselor talks to me, asks me how I feel, listens to me, treats me with gentleness and respect. He helps me feel good about myself and shows me that people are not all bad. As I begin to find safe people and trust again, I gain faith that I will recover.

*Today I will take a risk and ask a member
of my support group if I can call her
when I need support.*

I am learning to forgive.

My parents and I have not been close for years. I couldn't tell them when I got sick; one of them is a practicing alcoholic. They would not have believed, or accepted, my addiction—let alone my mental disorder. Still I missed them—I needed them—when I hit bottom.

In recovery, however, I feel differently about them. I see them now as people who have made mistakes, who have let me down, but who did for me what they could. Somehow I have renewed faith that each in their own way cares about me, and I can tell that I still care about them too. When I called them recently, it felt good just to hear their voices.

I will write out an affirmation that says,
"I can forgive. I can let go."

I am facing my powerlessness.

I'm following my co-occurring recovery plan, but for some reason, it doesn't seem to be working these days. I feel better for a while and then feel worse again (which makes me feel worse still). At times I wonder if I'll ever recover—and then I lapse into thoughts about giving up completely.

On the other hand, I wonder if I am expecting too much too soon. Or maybe I am trying too hard. Perhaps I simply can't see that I am, in fact, getting better because I'm so close to it. When I think about it this way, I leave myself some room for faith. Perhaps I just need to keep working my program and in time (my Higher Power's time), I will settle down and find a measure of peace.

I will pray for strength and call a friend
or sponsor for reassurance and support.

I need to keep "First things first."

In recovering from my co-occurring disorders, I have *two* "first things": *abstinence* in my addiction and *stability* in my mental disorder. I can't simply choose either abstinence or medication. I need to stay free of street drugs *and* keep taking my prescribed psychiatric medication. I can't simply choose between Twelve Step meetings or my group therapy meetings. They're different and I need them both, one for each disorder. Each part supports the other.

I must keep in mind that I have two no-fault disorders that can affect one another and so place my recovery at greater risk. I am coming to believe that my *very* first thing—the most important thing in my life—is recovery.

I will put my daily recovery activities first.

I want to stay abstinent.

When I was using, some days I'd wake up and look at myself in the mirror. I looked awful. I felt awful. I'd stare into my eyes and silently plead with myself to quit the drugs. I couldn't keep it up anymore. I was falling apart and things were falling apart all around me. I was scared. I no longer had control.

I'm grateful today that I finally became willing to accept this problem and that I finally got help. Sometimes I still feel like caving in, but there is something inside me that wants to hang on, wants to get better, wants to stay abstinent. I need to pay close attention to that desire.

> *When I feel like using again,*
> *I will tell a friend and ask for help.*

I am developing faith in my own experience.

When I first started having mental health problems, I did not know what was happening. I didn't have a clue about handling the problem or its source. It didn't help that family and friends understood even less.

When I realized that my moods were out of control, I got professional help. By and by, I got stable and began to accept my emotional life (although others still did not). I began to trust myself more and take greater responsibility for managing my disorders. I learned that I need not believe what others might say about my disorders and about what I feel or experience. With my time in recovery, I can simply believe in myself.

I will write about, or draw a picture of,
the most recent time I trusted my intuition.

I am coming to trust my feelings.

People tell me that I am different these days—lighter, more relaxed. I can hardly believe that I'm feeling pretty good now. A subtle change has taken place in me. And yet sometimes I can't trust it. I'm afraid that it will go away.

When I spoke about my confusion in group, I got some support. I learned that my fear of a sudden reversal will weaken in time as I get used to being successful. I learned that pride is not necessarily a bad thing and that it's OK to take note of my own healthy growth. I pray that my Higher Power will keep me humble *and* strong.

I will write out an affirmation that reads,
"It's OK to be strong and successful."

I continue to learn.

I know where I've been and I know where I'm going. I have had powerful emotions and powerful experiences. I have learned much and I am getting stronger all the time.

But I believe that there is more—more to feel, experience, and learn. Since there are always new experiences (and new interpretations of old experiences), I will strive to improve my understanding of myself. The point is not to be "recovered," but to embrace the process: the point is *recovering*. It is a transforming experience that teaches me to be open to whatever life brings.

I will welcome each day as a teacher.

I am honored to be called on to help.

Being a sponsor or support person offers two kinds of benefits. It helps a fellow traveler to recover.

And just as importantly, it helps me recover. Being a sponsor or support person (*a*) teaches me humility by reminding me of where I have been, (*b*) shows me that the more I give, the more I get, and (*c*) helps me understand myself better. In sum, lending support gives depth and meaning to my recovery.

Whenever I receive a call for help, I will
honor the request with my best self,
my fullest presence.

I need to let others help me.

I have never liked being ill and needing a doctor. Yet here I am, sick again. I wish I didn't need anyone's help or have to trust anyone. But I have co-occurring disorders and I am slowly realizing that I cannot manage these disorders on my own.

Maybe it's time I stopped resisting and started accepting. If I can't recover alone, I can at least take heart that there are many who can help: not just doctors but counselors, therapists, case managers, and social workers. And not just professionals, but caring fellow travelers and sponsors in support groups and Twelve Step fellowships. I can be grateful that help is available and that I am not alone.

I will pray for the willingness
to allow others to help.

I feel joyful.

I've been struggling over the past several months, first to get sober and then to get stable with my mental disorder: so much anger, fear, and frustration so much of the time.

But today, I feel grateful. My effort is paying off. I woke up feeling I had a handle on my life. I woke up with a feeling of strength, a feeling that I could accept and deal with whatever life offered me. It was a glow, a surge that said I truly want to be alive—right here, right now. I call this glow *joy*.

When I feel joy, I will humbly radiate it.
I will simply smile.

I need to take care of the basics.

In this process of getting abstinent and stable, sometimes I get so discouraged I hardly care about how I look. Sometimes even keeping my body clean and putting on clean clothes don't seem to matter much. Sometimes I simply don't take care of myself.

But I've learned that in everyday recovery from co-occurring disorders, taking care of basic hygiene really does make a difference. It helps me keep up my self-esteem and it helps me feel more at ease around people. Doing the basics for my body can help me stay balanced, avoid relapse, and generally be happier.

I will write down the basic ways I must take care of my body each day and then be sure to include them in my daily recovery plan.

I have new priorities.

Before recovery, I tried to soothe my mental health symptoms with alcohol and drugs. My first priority was to stop the pain. But instead of dealing with my problems and getting relief, I developed an addiction.

In recovery from co-occurring disorders, I am setting two different priorities that can help me heal: abstinence from addictive substances and stability with my mental disorder (regardless of which came first in my life). Both issues need attention, both at the same time, because each affects the other. As I deal with my problems, I will get relief. According to the Promises in the Big Book (pp. 83–84), my "whole attitude and outlook upon life will change," and I will "know a new freedom and a new happiness."

I will make a commitment to co-occurring recovery
by continuing to work with professionals (as needed)
and by teaming up with a sponsor and a support
person, one for each priority.

*My Twelve Step meeting is becoming
my foundation.*

I stopped using and got sober, but I lost my friends. I
wasn't stable yet and I felt like a mess. Often I found
myself feeling alone, angry, bored, and sorry for myself.
I wondered, How could a Twelve Step meeting help?
Nevertheless, I kept going for six weeks—just as the
program suggests for newcomers.

And then one day I realized the importance of this
meeting. First, I can rely on it like no one and nothing
else (holidays included). Second, it offers me fellowship
with people who share my experience, who understand
me, and who care about me. My meeting is the basis of
my recovery program, and I am deeply grateful.

*To strengthen my commitment to recovery
and my program, I will volunteer to do
service at my home meeting.*

I am bound to feel better.

This morning I woke up with bad dreams. My surroundings seemed strange. Then I remembered that I had dreamt I was back in treatment for my co-occurring disorders. I felt alone and shaky, just as I'd felt then.

And then I remembered a slogan I'd heard in group: *This, too, shall pass.* I said the words out loud. Then I repeated them silently: *This, too, shall pass.* It worked: my fear and anxiety lessened. Slowly I managed to get dressed, eat breakfast, and go about my morning's activities. I did my best to stay busy and let my thoughts be. This afternoon, I feel better. And what's more, I have just a little more faith that I can recover.

I will make an affirmation card that reads,
"This, too, shall pass."

I can hold on for at least this minute.

In the past, at the first sign of stress or anxiety, I would use drugs. Gradually, I used them regularly to *prevent* the return of anxiety. In the end, I could hardly stand even brief episodes of anxiety.

But this is changing now. In recovery from co-occurring disorders I am learning to accept my anxiety and to deal with it—especially since I've been abstinent. One technique I use is to break down time into manageable stretches. When I no longer have the strength to cope for the day, I pray for strength to cope for the hour. If sixty minutes becomes too much, I pray for courage and strength to manage for one minute. In the end, one minute is all I have to accept, one at a time. And with the help of my Higher Power, I can do it.

To hold on, I will say the Serenity Prayer
and distract myself with a physical activity.

I am not "crazy"; I have co-occurring disorders.

When I experience symptoms of my mental disorder, I feel embarrassed or ashamed—much as with my addiction. I don't want to see anyone or be seen. Often I feel misunderstood and rejected as well. Yet what I *need* is to feel accepted and understood.

I am not certain what the word *crazy* means to anyone else, but I cannot accept the term. I will not be called "crazy." I am a person who experiences two no-fault disorders, addiction and mental disorder. But first, *I am a person*—like everyone else.

I can become an advocate for myself and others with mental health disorders, and do something like joining the local chapter of the National Alliance on Mental Illness.

I want to stay willing.

When I finally realized I had to stop using, I knew it would be tough. I didn't want to stop. What would I do when I had symptoms of my mental disorder? What would I do with my time? (I felt empty just thinking about it.) Giving up using felt like losing a friend (and I had so few). I thought, *Haven't I had enough losses? Can I handle more pain and change?*

Yet drinking and using kept getting me into trouble and kept me sick. And I was finally tired of being sick. Quitting alcohol and street drugs let my meds work better—as my therapist always said it would—and *I* felt better. I see now how much abstinence has helped to accept my problem, trust my helpers, and begin a new life in recovery.

I will pray for the willingness to continue
accepting my addiction and working
my program to stay abstinent.

I lose control when I use.

I realize now that when I use, I forget to take my meds and go to support group meetings. Sometimes I even forget to eat or go to work. Basically, I don't seem to care what happens to me. I don't like myself. When I use, my mental disorder often gets worse. I'm glad I've stopped using again, and this time I want to *stay* stopped.

I used to think that drugs and alcohol were the only way I could survive. I thought I could use and still manage my life. But I can't. Using only makes me sicker. When I'm using, I'm not taking care of myself. I see now how powerless I am over my addiction. I want to stay abstinent. I think I can.

I will ask my Twelve Step group,
my support group, and my therapist
for help in staying clean and sober.

I can grow by telling my story.

In recovery, I no longer have to lie to myself or others. In telling my history of addiction and early recovery, as honestly as memory allows, I can practice coming to terms with my life, both the downs and the ups. I can show myself how ready and willing and able I am to practice the important principle of honesty.

In recovery, where I am both emotionally and spiritually safe, I have a chance to get rid of some of the guilt and shame about my life. I take advantage of this opportunity (and challenge) when I am honest about my past in the Fifth Step and honest about my present in the Tenth Step.

*Today I will practice honesty
in my Tenth Step review.*

OCTOBER

I can welcome the day.

I used to dislike mornings. When I would stay up late getting high, when I was out of work, when I didn't think I could bear another day of my mental disorder—I did not feel like starting the process all over again. I would burrow under the blanket as if to hide from the day.

With the help of my doctor, counselor, and support groups, I now have my disorders under control. These days my mornings are much better. Usually there are no nightmares, no hangovers, no hiding. I am glad for the new day and grateful for the energy to face it squarely.

Today I will say a prayer of thanksgiving
for my ongoing co-occurring recovery.

I am becoming more responsible.

Once a week I agreed to check in with my clinic and get a urine screen. I agreed to go to at least three Twelve Step meetings each week. I agreed to check in with my sponsor every day. I realize these are important, useful commitments, but I feel controlled; I feel as though I am unworthy of trust.

On the other hand, can I really be trusted these days? In the past I have promised to stay sober and then got high, promised to take my meds and then failed to even fill the prescription. It is hard to own up to, but maybe I need this structure for a while. And following through on these commitments will help me *earn* trust. Even though I resent it now, it may well help me to recover.

Today I will practice doing what I say I'm going to do. I will check in with my sponsor and take my prescribed medication.

I can trust again.

When I recall what I've been through in my life, I can see why it's hard for me to feel safe when I try to believe in someone. It seemed as if every time I let down my guard, I was mistreated or betrayed.

But eventually in recovery I have come to trust again. The process began with a person who was willing to accept *me*—regardless of my addiction and mental health disorder—a person who was relaxed, open, and consistent with me. My trust didn't come quickly; I tested him to see if I could feel safe. But gradually, it worked. I am grateful that my Higher Power gave me the strength to try trusting one more time.

Today I will take five minutes to think about how I can help my recovery by trusting myself and other people.

I will be taken care of.

Given a childhood of parental neglect—and then years of neglecting and abusing myself—I wasn't sure how much I really wanted to survive. I felt I had nothing and no one. Without faith or trust, I finally hit bottom—physically, emotionally, and spiritually.

And then something wonderful happened: I found the Twelve Step fellowship. I found people like myself, people who accept, understand, and care about me. I found a Higher Power and the Twelve Steps to guide me. I could never have envisioned these changes. They're gifts, and I am deeply grateful.

Today I will carry the message of hope.

I need relief from my guilt.

I feel bad about some things I've done in my life. Sometimes I feel I should be punished. This guilt is a weight I've lived with for many years. I used to try to forget it by drinking.

In recovery from co-occurring disorders, I've quit drinking, but I'm left with some unresolved guilt. It keeps me blue at times, keeps me angry at myself and others. It even increases my risk of relapse. But I'm learning a way to help ease that guilt. First I do a Fourth Step to learn exactly what I feel guilty about. Then I promptly do a Fifth Step to help release it. The good news from my fellow group members is that by doing these Steps I can look forward to some relief.

Today I'll make notes on the two things
I feel most guilty about and how
I can release this guilt.

I am a worthy person with two disorders.

A friend just canceled our date. I think it was partly due to my mental health issues, even though I'm stable and recovering. This hurts. Rejection always hurts, but especially when it is due to my co-occurring disorders, a pair of liabilities that are not my fault.

Still, I know I'm doing the best I can. I am working on my disorders—staying abstinent, going to therapy and Step meetings. I trust that I will be OK because I have a Higher Power and I know people care about me. Rejection hurts, but I am learning to deal with it.

*I will pray (or meditate) and share my pain
and sadness with a trusted friend.*

I am learning to accept, to say yes.

For a long time I kept hearing myself say no. For instance, *No, I am not an addict. No, I don't have mental health problems. No! I'll be fine if you'll just leave me alone.*

It's hard, sometimes very hard, but I am now learning to say, *Yes, I have co-occurring disorders.* Why? Because it's true. I have an addiction and a mental health disorder, and they have caused many problems in my life for some time. Now I am accepting my disorders and my need for help to recover. Now I want to get better. I am asking for help and receiving it. For all this I am grateful.

I will meditate on how good it feels
to stop denying my problems and
start working on them.

I can deal with painful memories.

All of a sudden I'll have a memory that really hurts, really scares me. It feels like a sock in the gut that knocks the breath out of me. I have to stop what I'm doing to collect myself. If the memories keep coming, sometimes I want to use.

But I cannot drink or take drugs. I must not. My recovery is too important to me. I've learned that if I use, I cannot deal with my memories or my other recovery issues. I know there is a better way than using. Abstinence is not easy, but it offers long-term relief and the chance to heal.

I will say the Serenity Prayer and use
physical exercise to help deal with
my painful memories.

I am coming out of denial.

At first I couldn't accept my counselor's concerns: In response, I said I didn't have a problem with drugs or alcohol and didn't need her kind of help (strike 1). I insisted that I didn't abuse substances—that I used them only to help me when I had symptoms of my mental disorder (strike 2). I insisted that I was managing my symptoms (strike 3). The facts, of course, were different. I was afraid, in denial, and I didn't understand myself.

Now that I have some time in co-occurring recovery (I'm stable *and* abstinent), I wish I had listened sooner to that addiction counselor. It has been hard admitting co-occurring disorders—both mental disorder *and* addiction—but since I did, I've felt better, especially through work in my Twelve Step fellowship. I now feel I am honest and no longer working against myself.

Today I will reread Step One in the Big Book and check in with my sponsor.

I feel cared about.

I didn't think I could talk about my problems. If I did talk, I wasn't sure anyone would listen or care. But I was sure hurting and desperate for relief.

By getting into treatment for my co-occurring disorders, I have found a way to get that relief. I now have a counselor and a support group. With their encouragement, I have found a Twelve Step group and a sponsor. Even all of these helpers cannot fix my problems, but they listen to me and they try to understand. They want me to feel better, and this makes all the difference. I no longer feel as alone, unknown, or unwanted—I am very grateful.

I will practice saying what hurts
in the supportive environment
of my helpers.

I can make my needs known.

When I experience symptoms of my mental disorder, my friends and family can sometimes make the situation worse. I think they get afraid—perhaps because they don't understand me or my problems. Sometimes they want to "fix" my problem (which is not appropriate) or else they expect me to just change the way I feel or behave (which is unrealistic).

In the past I've felt angry and frustrated about this sort of treatment. But now that I've had counseling for a while, I've learned more about my problems and especially about what helps me feel better and get stable again. For instance, when I'm having symptoms, I think I do better when, instead of a fix or a demand, I get some flexibility, a friendly ear, and an open mind.

I will write down two important needs when
I'm having symptoms and talk about them
with my counselor and a trusted friend.

I care about my health these days.

In the last few months before I hit bottom with my co-occurring disorders, I didn't care what I ate or whether I slept. In a way, my body was not important to me. I seriously neglected my health, especially with my addiction. In a way, I wanted to feel nothing.

But nowadays in recovery, I am paying my body much more attention. I am starting to forgive myself and thus make amends to my body. I am learning that along with spiritual and emotional work, I feel best when I support the physical work of my recovery too.

I will practice eating nourishing food today
and get some exercise.

*I need to take more responsibility
for my recovery.*

At first I didn't want treatment at all. I felt sorry for
myself because of my problems—I didn't like my moods
or the way I was drinking—but I wasn't willing to do
much about them. I didn't think they were serious.

But a trip to detox helped to change my mind. Finally
I could admit to my co-occurring disorders, and I could
face my need to deal with them. Nobody can recover
for me. My doctor or counselor or group or sponsor or
friends can offer guidance and support, but it is up to me
to follow through and make the changes. With the help
of my Higher Power, I will do what I need to do.

*I will meditate on how I can strengthen
and support my recovery.*

I am learning about a Higher Power.

I was OK with having a leader in my group at the clinic, but I didn't know about this "Higher Power" they talked about in my new Twelve Step group. I like to think I can take care of myself. I don't much trust people to do things for me. Besides, I haven't believed in God in a long time.

That was my initial reaction. But, as often happens, I'd overreacted. After a while, I learned that a Higher Power (or HP, "higher helper," or "source of help") doesn't have to mean "God." HP can mean almost anything—the group itself, an individual member, or simply my program. All I have to do is to believe that the power I've chosen is stronger than I am and that it can help me get better.

Today I'll take five minutes to think
about who or what is helping me
in my recovery.

I need to limit the stress in my life.

It's not fun, but I'm slowly learning how I create problems for myself in recovery. For instance, (a) I tend to make too many commitments, (b) I often try to do two things at once, and (c) I work too hard at my job. It seems I've managed to build a lot of stress into my life and left little time for myself and recovery.

Despite my time in recovery, I still need to make some changes or else face a setback or relapse. Making further changes in my lifestyle will be hard and I'll need help. But to stay on track in recovery—my most important job—I'll do what I need to do.

I will do some reading on Step Eleven,
review my priorities, and renew
my daily recovery plan.

I get help from many helpers.

I used to be afraid of asking for help. *Accepting* it was almost harder. But slips and relapses, setbacks and breakthroughs have taught me that I have needed (and still need) help. And slowly I've become more willing to ask for help *and* to accept it.

I feel stronger when I glance back and see that over time, help for my co-occurring disorders has come from many different people: men and women; young and old; recovering people (a sponsor, a support person, a host of friends) and professionals (a psychiatrist, a therapist, a counselor, a social worker, a caseworker, a clergyperson). I am grateful to them all.

*I will do the best I can on my own
and then respectfully call on my
helpers as needed.*

I think I think too much.

These days, I have several problems that I cannot solve. (It's like that with co-occurring disorders, I hear.) I work on them, but they aren't easy to resolve. Some days I just keep hashing them over and over. I can't let go. Soon I feel drained, anxious, and frustrated.

In talking with my sponsor about this painful spinning, I realized two things. First, it's in my nature to think and analyze. But being obsessed keeps me stuck and gets me nowhere. Second, as much as I want to be in control, I am not—my Higher Power is. The good news, however, is that I am developing a degree of faith. I have a sense that things will work out over time, whether I worry over them, feel bad about them, or not.

Today I will review Step Three and
clear my mind by writing out
a list of my problems.

I am slowly accepting my disorders.

Twelve months after my DUI and drug counseling, I still didn't believe I had a drug problem. It took a second DUI to convince me. Likewise, even after several months of therapy, I would not take my depression seriously. What finally changed my mind was crying uncontrollably and feeling suicidal.

Now that I have finally accepted both my addiction and my mental disorder, I have an idea about what took me so long. And yet, maybe I took just as much time as I needed—just long enough to feel bad enough to be willing to change. I trust that I won't have to wait so long in the future.

*Today I will practice acceptance
by allowing myself time to change.*

I am changing by letting go.

By going into treatment, I temporarily let go of my freedom and my home. I let go of time and money. In treatment I gave up old habits, old ways of thinking. I admitted my co-occurring disorders and started to change my life.

And in return for my willingness and effort, I have gained *true* freedom—freedom from addiction and from the symptoms and other effects of my mental disorder. In return, I have invested in an abstinent and stable future. I am learning new ways to cope, healthy ways to take care of myself. By admitting my co-occurring disorders, I am changing my life.

To help me learn from my thinking and
my process of growth, I will keep
a recovery journal.

I am practicing acceptance.

With my co-occurring disorders, sometimes I feel as if the rest of the world is passing me by. Right now I can only work part time, and I'm not happy with that. I often feel like I'm wasting my time. I live by myself in a studio apartment. I can't drive, so I have to take the bus when I go anywhere.

At times like this I focus on the idea that maybe my Higher Power has chosen a different path for me. I suspect the most important thing in my life these days is not career or family. It's recovery. By staying abstinent and stable, I will be on *my* path and all will be well.

I will say the Serenity Prayer and review
my list of assets (from Step Four).

*I need to know the difference between
street drugs and medication.*

When my psychiatrist first wanted to help me by prescribing a medication for my mental disorder, I said absolutely not. I told him I was in recovery from a substance use disorder and would take no mood-altering drugs. I said I was afraid of relapsing to my addiction. In a word, I couldn't yet trust him.

So I talked with someone I did trust, my sponsor in co-occurring disorder recovery. From her I learned that psychiatric medication is rarely addictive. And it differs from street drugs in several other ways: it is designed for specific disorders, given in strict dosages, and available only through a doctor and a pharmacy. Once I understood the difference, I was able to trust my psychiatrist with my co-occurring disorders. I could accept his treatment recommendations and make progress in recovery.

*I will make a list of the people I've come
to trust since I began recovery.*

I can handle my symptoms.

I can't stand it when I get this tension, this tightness, this buzz in my body. I can't settle down. What's happening to me? Why am I feeling this way? I'm sober now. What did I do to deserve this? I want this pain to stop.

As painful as the tension is, however, I know I can handle it. I can handle it because I'm not drinking over it; I'm not adding fuel to the fire. I can handle this attack because I'm not getting anxious about my anxiety. I am thinking clearly enough to recall that people can still have episodes of anxiety even though they're sober and taking proper medication—like me. I trust this won't last long and I can muddle through. When I need extra support, I will reach out to my helpers.

I will sit down and take four deep breaths
each minute for four minutes.

I can't do this on my own.

I remember thinking that using street drugs would take care of my mental health symptoms. I believed that the more I used, the better I would feel. I also believed that if I stopped using alcohol and drugs, my symptoms would worsen. I was wrong. One morning, I woke up feeling terrified. I suddenly realized that my "solution" wasn't working, and in fact, despite my self-medication, my problems were getting worse.

Now, in recovery from co-occurring disorders, I admit that I can't recover on my own, that I need outside help for my disorders. My first helper was a therapist who gently encouraged me to work with a Twelve Step group for my addiction. Later, I got help from a psychiatrist, and my doctor was helpful too. All three helpers—therapist, recovery group, and doctor—are powers greater than I am. I need them and I am fortunate and grateful to have them.

*In my prayers today I will remember
my helpers and all the help I am getting.*

I can cope.

It's not even dawn and I'm wide awake. I feel sad and scared and exhausted. After two weeks, my antidepressant still doesn't seem to be working. Right now, I'm wondering when I will ever feel better.

Still, my doctor said I might feel this way. He said it could take a couple weeks—maybe longer—for the medication to take effect. Coping is not easy, but I think I can still hang on. I have a Higher Power to help me. I will be better soon.

> *I will first ask my Higher Power*
> *for strength, and then I'll get out*
> *of bed and begin my day.*

I have found a better way.

I never expected to have a problem with alcohol and other drugs. But in trying to cope with the problems in my life, it became all too easy for me to rely on such a dangerous "tool." At the time, I didn't know a better way. I only knew I was in deep distress and looking for relief. I just kept using the wrong tool.

Since learning about addiction and mental health disorders, I have found a *better* way to deal with my life, and I am trying more useful tools to help me change. I'm seeing a psychiatrist who prescribed a medication for my mental health disorder. I'm using a counselor, a Twelve Step program, and a sponsor to help me work on my addiction and my emotional and spiritual problems. It's still not easy, but at least I'm working with the right tools.

I will read Step Two and thank my
Higher Power for all my helpers.

My mental health is improving.

For some time before I hit bottom, I struggled to cope with stress and painful emotions. Drugs and alcohol did not help me. But I couldn't admit any of this. To do so would have meant facing failure, feeling out of control, feeling "crazy"—even though I was doing the best I could, holding my life together on my own.

Perhaps I was in denial about my co-occurring disorders. But through going to therapy, reading educational materials, and getting personal support, I am learning that mental health is a matter of degrees. I am learning about myself and learning coping skills. I am putting my life back together, making it work even better than before.

I will take five minutes to meditate
on the ways I am OK.

I am exercising for my recovery.

Before I got into recovery I experienced numerous physical problems. For a long time I didn't know what was wrong. In a way, I didn't care.

But now in recovery, I care very much. Being in recovery from co-occurring disorders teaches me that addiction and mental disorders are also physical diseases. Just as I pray and meditate to help with my spiritual symptoms, and just as I go to Twelve Step meetings and counseling to help with my mental health symptoms, so too will regular exercise help my body. This is my physical recovery. If I exercise regularly, I will help repair any damage I've done and I'll be strong for each day's effort.

Today I will come up with a brief,
simple exercise routine I can
do every day.

I am letting go of blame.

My first response to learning I had co-occurring disorders was to ignore it. Then I didn't believe it. Then I denied it. As I came to see that I couldn't just wish these two disorders away, I looked for a scapegoat. If I had to suffer, someone or something was at fault. One by one, I blamed my disorders on my parents, family, job, God, bad luck—but mostly, and most hurtfully, I blamed them on myself.

But now, with a period of sobriety and stability, I see how little it matters who or what is to blame. What I experience are two no-fault biological disorders. What I am learning in my journey is that the more energy I concentrate on *recovery*, the healthier and happier I'll be.

I will pray to release myself
(and others) from blame.

I feel better when I stay active.

I remember one day when I first felt deeply depressed. I was sitting in a chair, overwhelmed and unsure how to cope. I sensed my dark thoughts getting darker. Eventually I could hardly move, hardly think. I felt paralyzed.

These days as I look back, I'm actually grateful for that experience—not because I enjoyed it, but because it still teaches me what to avoid. I now see that depressive symptoms are a signal for me to get active. I've learned that painful thoughts slow me down and that inactivity reinforces the pain. Action, however, helps keep my mind clear and gives me energy. To avoid getting bogged down in painful thoughts, I need to be physically active on a regular basis.

*Today I will be physically active
for twenty minutes.*

I need structure in my life.

As my co-occurring disorders got worse, my life came apart. Addiction changed my patterns of sleep; it even changed my priorities in life. With the depression that followed, I lost interest in taking care of myself. Eventually I lost most interest in my life.

But the daily routines of treatment helped. They showed me how putting structure back into my life supports recovery. With the help of my counselors, I worked out a recovery plan. Each day I set aside time to take care of my physical, emotional, and spiritual needs—my body, heart, and soul. Each day's plan is a little different, but all cover the basics I need to stay on track. I look forward to the benefits of structure.

*I will follow my plan closely to stabilize
my life and strengthen my recovery.*

I am practicing expressing myself.

One of the first things I learned in therapy for my mental disorder was *to express myself.* Keeping my feelings inside—which I have done for many years—can contribute to my disorder and keep me ill. To recover and stay healthy, I need to release my emotions regularly.

In therapy I also learned some different ways to express myself. For instance, I can talk about my feelings, paint them, or write about them (in a journal, in stories, or in poems). I could even sing or dance my feelings if I wanted to. I am grateful to have these tools that are helping me recover and stay healthy.

I will try a new tool today to see if it might help me express my current feelings.

NOVEMBER

I see now that I can get better in time.

When I realized I was sick, when I was first diagnosed with co-occurring disorders, I felt devastated. I wouldn't believe it. All I could foresee was more pain. And that scared me more.

But now that I've learned some things about my (no-fault) addiction and mental disorder, they scare me less. With the clarity that comes from knowledge and the passing of time, I see that my life *can* get better and I see *how* I can get back on track. As much as I wish all were well today, I accept that recovery will just take some time.

Today I will practice giving myself extra time
to do the things I need to do.

My appetite is returning.

It's been a while since I cared much about eating (this is not like me). My old favorites didn't appeal to me and trying new foods was out of the question.

But I am happy to report that my appetite is getting better. Recently I had a craving for a cookie—and sure enough, it tasted good. As much as I love cookies, I'm looking forward to regaining my interest in other foods too.

In my journal I will make a note of my two
favorite foods, my two favorite meals,
and one person I like to share meals with.

I am beginning to see I need help.

I used to wish everybody would just leave me alone about how much I was drinking or how I was acting. I thought, *Why should I get into treatment or go to Twelve Step meetings? I don't have a problem. And I don't like my friends for saying I do.*

I was angry. I felt like running away. I didn't like feeling rejected or being told what to do. But this was a little scary too. I had thoughts like, *What if my friends are right after all? What if I do have a problem? What do I do then? I'm upset. This is confusing. I need to think about this some more.* I still think this way sometimes. Now I know what I have to do.

Today I will call my sponsor or best friend and talk about what's going on with me.

I want to make new friends.

Because of my addiction and mental health problems, I don't have many friends—I gave up most of them. I got stable and sober, but *they* wanted me to keep using.

So now I'm trying to make new friends at my recovery meetings. Usually, I feel shy and awkward. I guess I'm afraid of them—no drugs to lower my inhibition—and maybe they're afraid of me. Yet I am tired of all my fear. I'm a good person who can be a good friend. Maybe it's up to me to break the ice.

I will pray for courage, and at my next meeting, I will start a conversation with a member of my group.

I want to let people know me better.

People ask me how I'm doing these days, but even if I could tell them, would they understand? At my support group, people often seem like strangers. Nobody knows me. Would they accept me if they did? I'm lonely.

It's hard for me to trust anyone right now. I'm afraid to let anyone get close. And yet people seem to want to help me. If I let them, maybe I could make friends. I know I would feel stronger and less lonely if I did. Maybe now is the time to let go of some of my fear.

At my next meeting, I will practice
being friendly and make eye contact
with other group members.

I need to stay active.

Before recovery, I'd get high whenever I felt bored. But now that I'm sober (and stable), drugs are no longer an option. It's especially hard these days when I feel edgy and restless, when I don't know what to do with myself.

The best answer I have right now is the Twelve Step fellowship. There, I'm not alone. I've heard others at my meeting say they've struggled with not knowing what to do with themselves or what to do with their time; many say they don't always know how to have fun. Through my program, I can stay in contact and stay active with safe, recovering people, as I slowly adjust to my new recovery lifestyle.

I will ask my fellow group members
what they do with their time and
how they have fun.

I am understood and cared for.

I have co-occurring disorders. My parents don't much understand my disorders. In fact, it feels as though they blame me for them sometimes.

This is why I am grateful for my recovering friends in both my Twelve Step group and my support group. They help keep me sober and stable. And through them I am coming to accept the fact that these disorders are not my fault—and not understood by many people. I trust that if I stick with my recovery plan, I will continue to get better and get out on my own again. I have a Higher Power who is helping me see to that.

> *Today I will meditate on my gratitude*
> *for all the caring people in my life.*

I need to be clean and sober.

Sometimes I think I'll never recover from my co-occurring disorders. I get scared and worry about losing my job. It is especially hard when it seems that no matter what I do, my mental health symptoms persist. At times, using seems like a tempting option.

But it's not. Even when my mental disorder feels unmanageable, I know that staying clean and sober helps. (*a*) It allows me to see myself (and others in recovery) gradually heal and change. (*b*) When the fear is strong, I don't act out. (*c*) Street drugs interfere with my medication. (*d*) I can pray. Sobriety, I believe, is helping me to get stable.

> *Today I will read Step One and*
> *attend a recovery meeting such as*
> *Dual Recovery Anonymous.*

I am not to blame for my two disorders.

What did I do to deserve the co-occurring disorders of addiction and mental disorder? Why must I have both disorders—isn't one enough? Sometimes I feel punished, as though I'd committed some crime.

I brought this up at my support group and was reminded that I don't deserve my disorders, didn't cause them, and cannot cure them. The group called them no-fault disorders and emphasized the importance of acceptance. It was a relief to hear that, although I am responsible for working on both disorders as best I can, I am not a bad person for having co-occurring disorders.

I will read about Step One and pray
for acceptance and strength.

I need to stay sober and stable.

At first I thought that if I just took my prescribed medication, I would be OK. I thought that if my mood got brighter and I didn't feel so restless so much of the time, I wouldn't have to drink.

But when my symptoms improved, I got a surprise— I found out I still wanted to use. I couldn't stop cold turkey; I *needed* to use. And my symptoms got worse after using. It's taken some time and some trial and error, but I now see that I must work on both disorders at the same time.

I will need a Twelve Step program
to deal with my addiction.

I can accept a breakthrough of my symptoms.

I used to get scared and angry when my mental disorder would "break through" my medication and produce strong symptoms. Sometimes I wanted to hurt myself. Often I would shut myself up in my room. I was ashamed for what felt like a loss of control.

Having a symptom breakthrough is still hard to accept, what with working a program of recovery from co-occurring disorders. However, I no longer feel so bad about myself when it happens. I have learned that even though I faithfully take my medication and go to meetings regularly for both my mental health and addiction, I am still powerless over my two no-fault biological disorders. I am not a bad person but a *recovering* person who is doing the best he can.

I will write out two ways I could help take care of myself if I experience a breakthrough of symptoms.

I can practice believing that "This, too, shall pass."

Before I got into recovery, I was vulnerable. I reacted sharply and quickly to my emotions, especially anxiety and anger. Without asking for help often—without even thinking—I got high. I managed my problems with street drugs. I didn't know there was any other way.

But in the program I'm developing a better tool—faith. When I have faith, the cravings pass in minutes. When I let go, I find help, twenty-four hours a day, through my Higher Power and sponsor. When I believe that "This, too, shall pass," it is easier to accept my disorders and the natural fluctuations of recovery.

*As soon as I have cravings, I will put
three program tools to work: the slogans,
the telephone, and prayer.*

I need more rest.

I have co-occurring disorders. That means I have a spiritual, emotional, and physical problem. These days I'm becoming more aware of the physical aspects.

I am still off the street drugs (and still feeling ill at times), taking medication for my mental health disorder (which makes me sleepy), and spending two nights a week in my two recovery groups (after putting in a full day of work). Working on mental health and addiction problems together takes a lot of energy. And I have a lot going on these days. I am glad that I'm active in my recovery—I'm feeling better and better—but I can tell now that I need more rest.

Tonight I will go to bed earlier than usual.

I can handle problems while they are still small.

Why am I so tired out these days? I come home at night and can hardly watch TV. I thought my recovery was on track, but I feel irritable and unfriendly. I also think I'm eating more than I need to. What's going on?

Come to think about it, my spouse and I still haven't settled some money matters. Then there's my new boss at work. And the car needs a tune-up and a muffler. Maybe *this* is what's going on. Maybe I've got a lot on my mind and it's starting to affect me. It's time to pay attention to these relapse warning signs, ask my Higher Power for help, and start dealing with my problems.

I'll use my nightly Step Ten inventory
to help monitor the stress in my life.

I do not want to be labeled.

If I had symptoms of my mental disorder in public, I would not want people to think, *He's crazy.* If I relapsed to my addiction in public, I would not want people to think, *He's a drunk* or *He's an addict.*

I am a human being. I am a valuable person. And I experience symptoms of mental disorder and addiction. I want to be known by my essence and my potential, not by my no-fault disorders.

> *I will write out a flash card that reads,*
> *"I am a valuable person in recovery*
> *from co-occurring disorders."*

I can forgive myself.

I want to learn to treat myself gently, as someone I love, not as someone I hate. I am proud of myself for beginning to change my life in the face of two disorders. I know that in my heart I seek health and wholeness. But I can't persevere—I can't recover—if I keep cutting myself down.

In recovering from my co-occurring disorders, I am bound to make some mistakes. If I can look at those mistakes for what they really are—reminders that I need to do something differently—I can avoid more guilt or shame and be kinder to myself.

*I will forgive myself for at least
two mistakes I made today.*

I can survive without street drugs.

With drugs, I could handle the ups and downs in my life and in my emotions—or so I thought. *Without* drugs, I see my real problems and feel my true feelings. By letting go of drugs, I've let go of something that gave me a great deal of control.

According to my Twelve Step group, my experience is not unusual (and early recovery is the hardest). I am learning that by working through the loss of my drugs and dealing with my feelings, my moods will lighten and stabilize. I'll sleep better. I will still have a mental health disorder that needs attention, but by staying sober, I'll know better what I need to do—and I'll be better able to do it.

I will take five minutes today to think
about two advantages I enjoy by
staying clean and sober.

I feel better when I share my story.

When I think about letting anyone know that I have both an addiction and a mental health problem, I'm afraid they won't understand or won't accept me. I'm afraid that they'll judge and abandon me.

Disclosing my struggle with co-occurring disorders is a risk. But my therapist is helping me by being a good example of a safe and trustworthy person. She respects me. She listens to me say what I need to say, in my own time. She shows me that I can still be accepted, no matter what I do or say. Through her, I am learning to let go and trust. When I talk about my story with *her,* I feel better.

*I will try "letting go" in my Twelve Step
meeting by sharing a little about
my ongoing recovery.*

I am enjoying a newfound balance.

When co-occurring disorders were undiagnosed and untreated, I reacted sharply to my fluctuating moods. I used alcohol and drugs to try to compensate. But I succeeded only in deepening my cycles and developing an addiction.

In recovery I feel as though I'm finally climbing off a teeter-totter. Instead of just reacting to changing moods, I am beginning to stabilize them and to maintain them. In the morning I exercise, meditate, eat, and go to work. In the evening I walk the dogs, eat, read or watch TV, talk to friends, and take my prescribed medication. At bedtime I pray. It's simple, it's structured, and it works.

I will thank my Higher Power for my progress
and tell my group about my routines.

I need to remind myself that "Easy does it."

When I first came to grips with my addiction and mental health issues, I thought a dozen Twelve Step meetings would cure me of my drug and alcohol problems. I thought that my psychiatric medication would quickly cure me of my anxiety and depression. I had no idea about the process and progress of recovery—the slips, the relapses, and setbacks.

But I am slowly recognizing that my expectations were unrealistic and naive. I see better now that I have several issues to deal with and that recovering will take some time. It doesn't help to expect perfection or to punish myself for mistakes. What *does* help, however, is to be very gentle with myself.

> *I will pray to understand, forgive,*
> *and accept myself.*

It will help if I let recovery "happen."

I was impatient when I first came into recovery. For example, once I got help with my mental health problems and joined a Twelve Step fellowship for my addiction, I thought I should feel better *now*. I wanted instant relief, instant recovery.

I still get impatient sometimes, but I am getting some perspective. Even with weekly therapy, coming to understand myself will take some time. Even with weekly Twelve Step meetings, my growth and my changes are subtle. I now see that recovery is a process, one that I need to *let happen*. Each day, I try to do what I need to do—knowing that I have time.

It will help if I practice doing
one thing at a time.

I don't have to work a perfect program.

I don't like the shame I feel for having co-occurring disorders. I want to recover as quickly as I can. At times I think I should be further along. And yet I will still forget a weekly therapy session, skip a meeting here and there, and get caught up in my old ways of coping. I've even had a slip with my addiction.

It's hard for me to accept my problems, but I need to gently remind myself that I experience two disorders that affect each other. I am new in recovery and there is no timetable. It will help if I can go easy on myself when I don't live up to my own (or others') standards. I know that I am making progress, especially when I can admit that I will continue to make mistakes.

> *When I do my Step Ten inventory tonight,*
> *I will take special note of my progress and*
> *pray to accept my weaknesses.*

I need to accept professional help to recover.

I was angry, ashamed, and frustrated about having to get treatment for my mental disorder (*and* for my addiction). It meant I couldn't take care of myself. It meant my disorders were serious. It meant loss of freedom.

And yet my symptoms were getting worse (using didn't help). With the two disorders together, it seemed managing on my own was too much. It's true, treatment was tough to face, but now I can see that it was for the best. I didn't like being there, but I *do* want to stay stable and sober.

I will pray to accept my need for ongoing help.

I can get support when I am afraid.

With my mental disorder, at times I think about abandonment, further losses, losing control, and never getting well. These thoughts scare me, and the fear can be crippling.

But I am grateful for a powerful phrase that often comes to my rescue: *No one ever died of fear.* It's miserable, debilitating, but not life threatening. The more I believe this, the more I can just say *I'm afraid,* the safer I'll be. The more I can tell someone I'm afraid, the less fear I'll feel, the less alone I'll feel, and the more help I'll be able to get.

I will work Step Two and come up with
one way I can help myself feel secure.

I say a prayer of thanks.

If I prayed at all in the past, it was only to make requests, not to give thanks. Thanks for what? My life was troubled and turbulent. I did not know where I'd been or where I was going. All I could see was brief relief in getting high (and the twinges of guilt and physical pain that frequently followed).

These days I am abstinent and stable. For the most part, I accept my disorders and their symptoms. I've come a long way in recovery. I still have plenty of problems in my life, but I am happier and healthier than ever before. Sometimes it feels like a miracle. I am deeply grateful to my Higher Power.

I will stop twice in my day to say
a prayer of thanks.

I am trying to accept others' lack of acceptance.

With a broken leg, there is a cast. With an appendicitis, there's a bandage and a scar. With my co-occurring disorders, there is no *visible* wound. So people often don't understand my pain and symptoms—for example, anxiety, depression, weight changes, or fatigue. They may not consider them real or legitimate.

Right now I am learning a critical lesson: I cannot change the way other people think or act. Fortunately, I can still get what I deeply need—certainly not from everybody and not from just anybody—but from my support group: (*a*) understanding and acceptance of who I am, (*b*) validation of my problems, and (*c*) support for my recovery.

> *Today I will pray to accept myself*
> *and pray to accept the people*
> *who don't accept me.*

I need to express my emotions.

I don't like the way I'm feeling these days. I don't like having to cope with my addiction and the strong emotions that come with my mental health disorder. Right now I don't like myself. I don't like the way my life is going. I'm discouraged, frustrated, and angry.

When I called my sponsor, he understood. He said that at one time, he had felt the same way. Then he offered me a suggestion, one he still uses today: with strong and painful emotions, look for a way to safely express them—whether with words or images or actions. I thanked him and agreed to give it a try.

Today I will practice expressing my feelings in two ways: once by myself with words, images, or actions and once with a friend.

I am no longer avoiding my problems.

In the past I had a ready solution to any upset or problem—I'd get high. It seemed to work, at least for a while. But instead of teaching me how to face problems, it taught me how to avoid them.

To begin changing this old way of coping, I got clean and sober. In recovery I am now learning new coping skills, such as reaching out for help, going to support group, and journaling. Although the skills still feel tentative and unfamiliar, I no longer feel helpless. I now have some choices. And when I have choices, I have less fear and more strength.

Today I will practice a new skill
on an old problem.

*I am becoming more tolerant
in life and recovery.*

When I was using and having symptoms, I had little patience or tolerance. I couldn't wait for a red light to change or a deposit to clear the bank. I wanted what I wanted when I wanted it. I reacted sharply and quickly. I was headstrong.

With some time in recovery, I have more patience. I can think things through. I am less irritable and fearful. Getting clean and sober has helped a lot. So has taking my medication. I am finding out that there are no quick fixes and that it helps when I take my time.

*Today I will practice walking slower
and driving slower.*

I know that abstinence is critical in my life.

In the process of hitting bottom, I could think of little else than making sure that I drank and stayed drunk as much as possible. In a way, I believed using was keeping me alive. I knew no other way to deal with my physical or emotional problems.

My daily goal in recovery is the opposite—my life depends on staying clean and sober. Abstinence is my principal tool for dealing with problems. And with the help of my Higher Power, I can do what it takes to stay abstinent.

I will write a note to myself about the most
important thing I must do today to stay
abstinent and carry it with me.

DECEMBER

I am finding my strength.

I am having a setback with my mental disorder. There is a storm in my brain. I am afraid. I am frustrated, furious, and exhausted. I go to group, do therapy, take my meds, and still I feel hopeless and helpless.

Yet in my heart, I know I have a Higher Power who cares about me—my sponsor checked in with me twice yesterday, and today I have an emergency appointment with my therapist. I know, too, how much progress I've made in recovery, and I believe this setback is not my fault. My job now is to weather the storm.

I will ask my Higher Power for strength
to stay with my daily recovery plan
the best I can.

I want to be known.

These days I want to tell my recovery story. It's not that I'm proud of my mental health and addiction problems. It's not that I want people to pity me. In fact, I tend to feel shy in front of a group (even when some are my friends).

But these days I *need* to tell my recovery story. I want people to know me, to understand me better (I want to understand *myself* better). Now, more than ever, I need a safe place; I need to belong.

At my next meeting I can offer to tell my story.
I'll be honest, authentic, and brief.

I am slowly accepting the process.

When I first heard of using the Twelve Steps for my addiction, I presumed that after twelve meetings I'd be cured. And I thought that with medication (the first one prescribed), my mental health symptoms would vanish. I am finding out, however, that recovery doesn't work this way—and that I am impatient. I want to get better—and I want it *now*.

What I'm learning instead is that time is a healer and recovery a process. To stay in recovery and avoid relapse to addiction or mental disorder, I need regular counseling, carefully prescribed medication, and continuing attendance at Twelve Step meetings.

> *I will write out this affirmation and*
> *carry it with me: "I am recovering*
> *one day at a time."*

My meds are not street drugs.

I have co-occurring disorders. I've been sober for a couple of months, but my psychiatrist now suggests that I take a medication to help me with my rage and shifting moods. I can see I need this help, and I want to feel more like myself again. But as a recovering alcoholic, I'm terrified about taking drugs.

So I talked to my sponsor from my co-occurring recovery group. She explained the critical difference between medication and street drugs: medication is prescribed by a doctor, for a specific problem, at a specific dosage, for a specific length of time—and carefully monitored all the while. She also pointed out AA's supportive pamphlet *The A.A. Member—Medication and Other Drugs: Report from a group of doctors in Alcoholics Anonymous.* I'm glad I talked with my sponsor. It helped.

*I will get a copy of the AA pamphlet
and read it carefully.*

I am learning to admit a mistake.

When I make a mistake, it's hard for me to admit it. I get mad at myself (or mad at everyone else). I get embarrassed and feel ashamed. Sometimes I fear rejection or punishment, even when the mistake is small.

But my Twelve Step program is helping me. At meetings, I regularly see people admitting their problems, acknowledging their flaws, and talking about mistakes they've made during the week. I see that it's OK to make a mistake, that it's OK to admit it, and most of all, that doing this *helps.* I am learning that this program is about forgiveness.

*Today I will look at myself in the
mirror and admit one of my
mistakes to myself.*

My life is changing.

I look around me and nothing looks the same—although nothing physical has changed. It's the same city, family, home, and job. But it doesn't feel the same. *I don't feel the same.* Sometimes, I feel a little lost.

According to my counselor, there may be two major changes at work: (*a*) I am no longer drinking and (*b*) I am now taking medication for my mental health disorder. He also pointed out that I am attending a support group and a Twelve Step meeting, and I'm meeting new people. He admitted that with all these changes, he might feel a little lost too.

> *I will list three anchors—whether people,*
> *places, or things—that help me stay*
> *centered in my recovering life.*

I need to take my meds.

I know I have co-occurring disorders, although I don't like to admit it. I know I need to take medication for my mental disorder, although it has taken a while to accept it and its side effects. I know that the medication helps me relax, think more clearly, and generally get on with my life. But lately, I keep forgetting to take it.

I am not sure what is going on with me, but I am scared and don't want it to get out of hand. To remain stable (and abstinent) in recovery, I need to talk about this with my therapist and my Twelve Step recovery group. I need their experience and support.

I will post reminders to take my medication
and ask a friend in recovery to
confirm it once a day.

I can smile again.

My co-occurring disorders have kept me down. Things were serious at times—I was desperate, despondent, and out of control. Nothing was fun, not even getting high (that just diminished the pain, though it didn't last).

With treatment, however, I am feeling better. Since I was able to admit my problems and ask for help, I am no longer alone in my struggle. I am with people who understand, many who even have co-occurring disorders themselves. I now feel hopeful. Change looks possible. These days I find myself smiling at people and looking forward to simple pleasures.

In my journal I will write about two events
that made me happy today.

I am learning to pray.

Before I started learning about the Twelve Steps in my recovery program, I did not pray. I did not have talks with a Higher Power. I was angry and I felt too alone and unloved to trust. I could not admit that I needed help, although I needed it badly.

Now, after only a few months in recovery from co-occurring disorders, I have already seen prayer work for others. By quiet example, they are teaching *me* how to pray—simply, personally, any time, any place. I can now admit to my Higher Power that I need help. And I feel strong enough to ask for that help in a spiritual way. I am learning the power of prayer. I believe mine will be heard.

I will stop whatever I am doing,
close my eyes, and make contact
with my Higher Power.

I know now that I find no relief when I drink.

I tried to handle my deep sadness and anxiety by using alcohol. When I drank, I paid less attention to my feelings. (In fact, I seemed to have fewer feelings.) But when the drug's effects wore off, the deep sadness and anxiety remained. I also had guilt and shame and a headache. All this pain—and still I wanted to drink again.

Now in recovery when I have painful feelings, with the help of my Higher Power, I don't drink—it would only increase the pain. I don't try to erase the feelings. As best I can, I let them be and apply the tools of the program. Slowly, eventually, the pain lessens. Slowly, I heal. When I abstain, I can find relief.

Because urges tend to pass in four or five minutes,
I will try counting slowly to 300.

I am getting used to my meds.

I thought that taking psychiatric medication would help fix my problems, not cause them. While it has helped with my mental health problems, the price is some unpleasant side effects. I don't like having a sensitive bladder, a limited diet, a dry mouth, or some temporary sexual problems.

But lately I've come to see that these discomforts are minor compared to the disasters caused by my mental disorder. Deep down I am grateful that medications exist that can help me cope and adjust. I can learn to live with some side effects.

Today I will look for a positive aspect of
two negative situations in my life.

I have not one but two disorders.

I knew I had a problem with drugs—I kept losing jobs by going to work high. But it wasn't until later, when I finally got into treatment, that my doctor diagnosed my mental health disorder.

In treatment I learned that I have *two* no-fault disorders: addiction *and* depression. I learned that I need to stay clean and sober, *and* I need to stay stable with my mental disorder. To do this I am now taking medication and learning healthy ways to cope with the symptoms of my biological disorder. It's hard to accept having co-occurring disorders, but now that I know what my problems are, it is easier to do what I need to do to recover.

*I will attend a Twelve Step meeting
that supports recovery from co-occurring
disorders and stay in touch with my
personal and professional helpers.*

I know what I need to do.

Some days I wonder, *What did I do to deserve these co-occurring disorders?* Sometimes I am hard on myself and think, *People don't get this sick without a reason.* With thoughts like these, I feel ashamed and guilty.

But in recovery I need to counteract these messages. It helps when I recall a most important lesson: Even though I may feel bad, and even though it feels like people may treat me differently, *I am not a bad person. I do not deserve my two disorders. They are not my fault.* Instead of giving in to guilt, fixating on the negative, my task is to work my recovery program daily, to simply do the best I can.

*Today I will make a list of all the
steps I am taking to recover
from my disorders.*

I want to show my gratitude.

When I was experiencing strong symptoms of my mental disorder and using street drugs every day, I was angry at the world for my problems and angry at myself because I couldn't fix them. I felt grateful only when I could get high and find some relief from pain.

These days, it's different. I feel deeply grateful to my helpers and my program because I'm abstinent and my mental health symptoms are in check. I feel acceptance, strength, and much goodwill. I want to give back to others with co-occurring disorders some of what I've recently received. I want to help carry the message of hope and recovery.

I will do two acts of kindness today:
one for a stranger and one for myself.

I can change.

When I was using, I did not like how I felt or how I behaved. I suppose I continued to use because (*a*) part of me always believed it would be different the next time, (*b*) it was familiar, and (*c*) I thought it kept me safe (even though it caused serious problems at the same time). When I got into recovery for co-occurring disorders, I just wanted relief from my mental health symptoms, my emotional pain. I wasn't looking to become a "better" person.

And yet through recovery meetings, therapy, and short-term medication, not only do I feel relief, but I am growing and developing as a person. I feel it especially as I work Step Seven and ask that my shortcomings be removed. I am *open* to change. I don't know how I'll change through this Step, but I trust my Higher Power that all will be well.

I will write out the Seventh Step Prayer
(p. 76 in the Big Book) and carry it with me.

I am gaining some perspective.

I was feeling angry and sad, so I got together with some friends. I thought that simply being with other people would help. But I still felt empty and distant. To top it off, I started feeling sorry for myself because I didn't get what I wanted or expected. And then I felt guilty because I wasn't much fun to be around.

But after meditating for a while, I saw my emotions in a different light and I realized three things: (*a*) *Because* my friends were willing to get together with me, I know they accept and support me. (This idea feels good.) (*b*) Maybe I can't "fix" my moods; maybe I need to accept them for a while. (I don't like this notion, but it helps to be realistic.) (*c*) Even though my expectations were not met, I learned something. My attitude is changing for the better.

The next time I feel bad about something
I've done (or not done), I will take a time-out
to meditate and improve my perspective
and self-understanding.

I want to succeed.

I've tried to stop using alcohol and drugs many times on my own, and I've tried many ways. Here I am again, looking at yet another way, the Twelve Step fellowship. Sometimes I wonder, *What's the use? Why should I believe that this will work any better than the others?*

Yet from what I've learned about the Steps in talking with my therapist about my using and recovery, I feel more open and willing. I've learned that: (*a*) The Twelve Step program is considered especially helpful for people with addiction. (*b*) At recovery meetings for people with co-occurring disorders, for example, I would be with other people who experience and understand my addiction and mental health problems. (*c*) At meetings, there's no requirement (except to listen) and I will not be judged. (*d*) Since I'm tired of going it alone and failing, I might as well give the fellowship a try.

I will make a commitment to attend
six Twelve Step meetings and give the
program a chance to work for me.

I am sick and I need help.

I remember when I finally hit bottom. As hard as I tried, I couldn't seem to stay clean and sober. Nor could I ward off my sadness any longer—even by using. I felt like I was losing ground. My strength was low.

Odd as it sounds, even then I sensed this wasn't all bad. I was exhausted from struggling and losing; I had done all I could. I felt I was finally willing to give up (in a way)—especially my pride—and accept that I couldn't do this on my own.

I will continue to ask friends or doctors
or counselors for the help I know I need.

I am slowly accepting my need for medication.

When my therapist first suggested it, I rejected the idea of taking psychiatric medication. I didn't want to feel weak by using a drug to handle an emotional problem. I didn't want to feel like I was "crazy." I got angry at her for merely suggesting it.

It wasn't easy to face, but eventually it all became clear to me: I've tried hard, but I can no longer handle my mental health symptoms on my own. In fact, I am tired of trying. But I don't want to feel weak, ill, and ashamed. Maybe I can look at taking a psychiatric medication like taking a medication for *any* disorder I might experience.

> *I will go for the medication assessment*
> *and fill the prescription if one is given.*

I want to laugh more.

Being sick is no fun. I didn't have a great sense of humor *before* I got sick. I'd hate to lose what I had.

In coping with my co-occurring disorders, it has been difficult for me to be anything but serious. But when I'm given a little nudge, when I get just a little perspective, I can see that I'm too wrapped up in my pain—I haven't laughed in weeks. I want to change that. Humor—as I faintly recall—really feels good. It loosens me up. I forget about myself for a moment or two. It makes my life easier somehow (even when I feel like being somber). I could say that humor is therapeutic—but that would be taking it too seriously.

Today I will remember how good I feel when
I laugh. I will look for the silly, the witty,
the lighthearted, the absurd in my day.

I can do one positive thing today.

For a long time I was stuck in a rut. I kept having symptoms, getting high, cutting back, then having symptoms again—over and over. I had little strength or desire to change my ways. Doing anything different was frightening.

Even with some time in recovery from co-occurring disorders I still find that change is hard, but it's getting easier. What helps the most is when I manage to do one small thing different in my life—*just one thing*—that I set out to do that day. Then I feel that I am making change, making progress. Change happens one step at a time. My task is to keep taking these steps, however small.

I will write down one small thing I can do today to make change in my life—and then do it.

I can stay well if I stay sober.

I feel the urge to drink. I haven't used in several weeks, but the urges still come. Sometimes it's hard to resist them, especially when my problems pile up and I can't see how they will ever get resolved.

What helps me at times like this is to recollect how far I've come in my recovery. I'm not only sober these days, but with the help of my psychiatric medication and counseling, I am stable. Since I have been able to get a handle on my symptoms, I'm thinking more clearly and I can concentrate on what I need to do to recover. I don't feel so vulnerable. If I gave in to an urge now, I'd lose my sobriety *and* I might interfere with how my meds work. For recovery from co-occurring disorders, I need sobriety *and* stability.

> *Today I will meditate on how my life*
> *has improved since I got abstinent.*

I am calming down.

Before I got help for my anxiety, I used to feel frantic at times. I'd sit down, then get up. I'd pace. Down. Up. Pace. I couldn't settle down. And I couldn't stop thinking or worrying.

Things are better now. I've admitted my problem and I'm letting others help me (a caring therapist and a support group). I am learning that my problem includes fear of feelings and trying to avoid them. So in a safe environment, with people who have problems like mine, I'm learning to accept my feelings and deal with them constructively. This helps me relax and I am grateful.

I will write down two coping techniques
on a card and keep it handy
for times of stress.

I miss my family.

Before I got clean and sober and stable, I avoided my family—parents, brothers, and sisters. I was afraid of what they would say to me about my drug use or about my mental health issues. I was in denial. I was protecting myself and I know I hurt them (and hurt myself as well).

These days, I realize how much I miss them. Of course, I want them to see how much better I am. But most of all, I want to ask them for their forgiveness—as well as their support. I need my family back.

I will ask my therapist to help me
reconnect with my family.

I have hope.

Dealing with a mental health disorder, my life felt painful, confused, and out of control. Dealing with an addiction at the same time was harder still: what I took for a solution to my mental pain only turned out to make things worse. In time I lost faith in myself.

But my friends did not. Eventually they helped me to see my serious problems and later to get treatment for them. Soon I felt I had a chance. Soon I *believed* I could change. With all the help I'd been given, *I felt hope*, and my faith began to return.

*In my prayers today I will ask
for the willingness to change
and be changed.*

I don't have to go it alone.

I had no idea how much emotional and spiritual pain I was in. I knew I felt depressed about my life—and I knew I was staying high a lot of the time—but I couldn't see my basic problems. I was just trying to manage on my own despite the problems the drugs were causing at work and at home.

One day I woke up and realized I could no longer manage on my own—I admitted to myself that between drugs and my moods, I had a serious problem. Later, I admitted it to a trusted friend. After a period of painful soul-searching, eventually I found a Twelve Step meeting, then a therapist, and finally a sponsor. Together, they have changed my life. In recovery, I have found relief. I will no longer go it alone.

This week I will thank my helpers
and I will practice being open
about my feelings.

I try to accept people who don't accept me.

My co-occurring disorders are a difficult, awkward, and troublesome pair of disorders. Some people don't think I'm really sick. Others do think I'm sick and avoid me. Either way I can feel rejected, defensive, and ashamed.

But *I* know the nature and significance of my disorders, and I am learning to manage them. I suppose it's not surprising that some people wouldn't understand or accept me and my particular set of problems. But these people do not live or make choices about my life—*I* do. And I am happier and healthier when I choose how much their opinions will affect me.

I will get support when I feel stigmatized
and then concentrate on working
my recovery plan.

I need to learn about my relapse triggers.

I feel at a loss. I'd been clean and sober for a while, but then I slipped twice and I don't really know how it happened. As best I can recall, I got very upset about something and the next thing I knew, I was feeling the guilt and ache of withdrawal.

In my group it's a good thing that we're learning how important it is to prevent a relapse from happening. This means finding out on my own (or with outside help) (*a*) the things I think or do that put me at risk for using and (*b*) the things I think or do that immediately endanger my recovery. I want recovery, and these days I am willing to go to any lengths to get it.

*I will write down my two most dangerous
triggers for slips and relapse and discuss
them with my sponsor and counselor.*

I am working on my fear of people.

I tend to be afraid of people. For one thing, I can't seem to trust much yet. I'm also afraid to talk. I don't know what to say and I think I'll make a fool of myself. Mostly, I'm afraid that they won't like me. It's hard for me to make friends, hard to feel safe, hard to relax. And easy to feel alone.

But with the help I am getting for my mental health problems—*and* my drinking—I feel better. I am learning that I am a worthwhile, likable person and that I'm not as different as I thought I was. The best part is that *I am not alone:* I'm meeting others who feel as I do and are working a program of change.

I will practice smiling at myself in the
mirror and saying "Hi!"

I feel much better about myself these days.

For some time, my mental health disorder and addiction affected each other. A setback in my mental health symptoms was usually followed by a relapse to my addiction; relapse was followed by a new setback. I could not deal with both disorders at the same time. I felt trapped in a downward spiral and I felt I was a failure.

But getting into recovery from co-occurring disorders has reversed that spiral, one day at a time. With the help of my Higher Power, I am coming to accept myself and the recovery process. I am working a Twelve Step program and getting help for my mental health disorder. Merely facing my two disorders was tough, but I am proud of how far I've come. These days I feel renewed strength and confidence.

I will practice keeping notes on my
stages of growth; they will give me
courage in the future.

I am learning about bad drugs.

Now that I'm clean, I can see what bad drugs really are. They're the ones where each time you buy them the seller changes, the price changes, and the package changes. Often, even their effects change. Such drugs I now call "street drugs," and I don't use them anymore.

The only drugs I use come from a pharmacy. Their price, package, and effects are consistent. I call them "medicine" or "medication." My medication is prescribed for me by my doctor, and I take it according to strict instructions.

At my next recovery meeting for co-occurring disorders I will share my old and new understanding of bad drugs.

About Hazelden Publishing

As part of the Hazelden Betty Ford Foundation, Hazelden Publishing offers both cutting-edge educational resources and inspirational books. Our print and digital works help guide individuals in treatment and recovery, and their loved ones.

Professionals who work to prevent and treat addiction also turn to Hazelden Publishing for evidence-based curricula; digital content solutions; and videos for use in schools, treatment and correctional programs, and community settings. We also offer training for implementation of our curricula.

Through published and digital works, Hazelden Publishing extends the reach of healing and hope to individuals, families, and communities affected by addiction and related issues.

For more information about Hazelden publications,
please call **800-328-9000**
or visit us online at **hazelden.org/bookstore**.

Other Titles That May Interest You

Sane
Mental Illness, Addiction, and the 12 Steps
MARYA HORNBACHER

Marya Hornbacher, author of the international best sellers *Madness* and *Wasted*, offers an enlightening examination of the Twelve Steps for those with co-occurring addiction and mental health disorders.

Order No. 3029

Find Your Light
Practicing Mindfulness to Recover from Anything
BEVERLY CONYERS

Author Beverly Conyers—one of the most respected voices in wellness and recovery—has guided hundreds of thousands of readers through the process of recognizing family roles in addiction, healing shame, building healthy relationships, releasing trauma, focusing on emotional sobriety, and acknowledging self-sabotaging behaviors, addictive tendencies, and substance use patterns. With her newest work, Conyers shows us how the practice of mindfulness can be a game-changing part of recovering from anything and everything.

Order No. 3591